THE LYNCHER IN ME

THE LYNCHER IN ME

A SEARCH FOR
REDEMPTION IN THE
FACE OF HISTORY

WARREN READ

BOREALIS
BOOKS

Borealis Books is an imprint of the Minnesota Historical Society Press.

www.borealisbooks.org

The Minnesota Historical Society Press is a member of the Association of American
University Presses.

Manufactured in Canada

10 9 8 7 6 5 4 3 2 1

∞ The paper used in this publication meets the minimum requirements of the
American National Standard for Information Sciences—Permanence for Printed
Library Materials, ANSI Z39.48-1984.

ISBN-13: 978-0-87351-607-5 (cloth)
ISBN-10: 0-87351-607-9 (cloth)

LIBRARY OF CONGRESS CATALOGING-IN-PUBLICATION DATA

Read, Warren
    The lyncher in me : a search for redemption in the face of history / Warren Read.
        p. cm.
    ISBN-13: 978-0-87351-607-5 (cloth : alk. paper)
    ISBN-10: 0-87351-607-9 (cloth : alk. paper)
    1. Lynching—Minnesota—Duluth—History—20th century. 2. Duluth
(Minn.)—Race relations—History—20th century. 3. Duluth (Minn.)—Biography.
4. Read, Warren, 1967– —Family. 5. Read, Warren, 1967– —Childhood and youth.
6. Family secrets—Case studies. 7. Redemption—Case studies. 8. Read, Warren,
1967– —Travel—West (U.S.) 9. West (U.S.)—Description
and travel. I. Title.
    HV6462.M6R43 2008
    364.1'34—dc22   2007044847

PICTURE CREDITS
p. 98, bottom: Courtesy of the Kansas State Historical Society
p. 99: Minnesota Historical Society Collections
p. 104, top: Josephine Lawrence Collection, 1844–1896,
    Western Historical Manuscript Collection–Columbia, Missouri
Photograph of rope for part titles by Craig Davidson
All other photos Read collection

Evil is unspectacular and always human,
and shares our bed and eats at our own table.

W. H. AUDEN

The following memoir is a work of nonfiction. The people depicted in the book are, or were, living and have been illustrated to the best of my recollection or, in the case of historical figures, by thorough research. In some cases, the names have been changed to protect the identity of a living person not connected with the publication of this book or whose family members might be negatively impacted by the person's depiction. All historical figures are recounted according to researched documents; no names have been changed in those cases.

THE LYNCHER IN ME

ONE

Two men are back to back, their bodies slightly touching just at the elbows. A thick wooden pole stands between them, beginning just behind their heels and rising up above their heads, disappearing from the frame of the postcard. Bare skin, arms restrained by their own torn shirts, they are the centerpiece of a gratuitous, macabre portrait.

Lines of white rope encircle their necks; a crescent of even whiter faces surrounds the hanging bodies in a proud display of heroic conquest. They are scarecrows nailed to a tree, hovering just inches above the ground. Of the dozens of bystanders in the scene, only one is smiling unabashedly—a brilliant, ecstatic grin that is all the more incongruous when one notices, nearly touching his right shoe, the head of a third victim, his body lying in a pummeled heap at the man's feet.

I've been among people who I'm sure would sooner see me dead than living with another man and I know that there are times and places that I might be discovered hanging from a hastily fashioned noose or tied to a barbed-wire fence, enveloped by men and women who see me not as a human being but as a category, an aberration, an epithet. I take in the seething hatred in the photo, the objectification of a human being set apart from the masses, and I know that as far-removed as I am from the men beaten and lynched that night long ago, I am not so different.

A shift in my perspective and I'm scanning the figures in the image for something else entirely. The faces surrounding the dead men are stoic, satiated; a few even look uncomfortable. I search apprehensively for the familiar, peering at heads that crane above the crowd, men vying to be captured by the photographer's lens. There is one whose frown could be my mother's and my heartbeat falters. Another one has my eyes. A blurred figure just on the edge of the frame has the prominent nose that I've come to recognize as my relation, but the jawline isn't right. This jaw is soft, not squared and chiseled as if from granite and once again I am relieved. It's not him. I am pulled into the muted imagery of the crowd and before I know it, I become lost trying to force the past into the present. What I am seeking exists somewhere in that photo and I know that as far removed as I am from the men standing in that crowd eight decades ago, I am not so different.

I imagine that I might crawl into the scene, like a photographic version of Alice's looking glass. And from my vantage point some eighty years later and a thousand miles away, I could actually be in Duluth, on that June night of 1920. I would walk among the mob, passing between them, and perhaps then I would see all sides—the trembling arms, the sweat along the backs of their necks, the deep scratches on the edges of their shiny black boots—and maybe then their evil would become less potent. I would ask them, is this what you really wanted all along? When the morning light shines down on this corner will you return to stand again in smug satisfaction? I would move into the headlights' beam and stand at the post, reaching out to touch the hands of the murdered, and I would promise them that one day they would be raised again, only this time in admiration and atonement. Then I might turn and go beyond the camera's eye, back down Second Avenue to the battered jailhouse with its bricks scattered in the street among shards of broken window and maybe there I would find him and I would finally be able to ask, "Pa, do you know what you have done?" And when I take his hands in mine I would show him, make him see the blood, show him that the blood covering his hands has traveled three lifetimes to stain the hands of his descendants. And maybe then he would tell me what I need to hear.

CHAPTER 2

I CROUCHED BEHIND THE BUSHES; spines of holly leaves scratched the sides of my face. A wild throw and both my ten-year-old son Dylan and I were digging through the one spot in the garden I'd hoped not to have to search for a baseball. Still I smiled confidently, knowing that if nothing else, my son wasn't afraid to be where he was, by my side, seeking to correct a less-than-perfect effort on his part.

On a night not too long ago in the relative realm of generational time, when I was just a few years older than my son is now, a holly bush of this size would play a completely different role for me. Its invasive scratch on my skin would be a strange comfort, dancing ever so lightly against the flesh. The holly bush then was an irritating reassurance of camouflage, safety from him, a man whose life would have been much less complicated with me, his wife's burdensome young son, out of the picture. I scraped the dirt aside as my son asked again if I'd found the ball. I told him no, we'd keep looking, while in my private thoughts I remembered how, twenty-five years earlier, in the cover of the thorny brush, the Rolodex of escape routes had spun wildly in my mind, each card coming up frustratingly empty. What the hell could I have done then? Run away? To where? Even today, I try to reach back to reassure a scared adolescent who has long since grown to adulthood that there was nothing else he could have done but hide and wait. My lip had begun to swell; a taste of iron, blood leaking from my mouth. *Mom can't ignore this,* I'd thought, *not this time.*

It had been a school night for me, another work night for my stepfather Lenny; he'd gone to the Kozy, or maybe the Townhouse, again. Most times he'd stumble in after last call, lurching right past my room, and pay me no notice, no reason to stop by the bedroom just off the living room. On this night, he didn't go on up to bed with my mother. He came back for me.

"Get up and get out here."

I stood in my underwear, squinting from the backlight of the kitchen ceiling fixture that hovered over his bobbing head like a dingy halo. His raggedy body swayed and the noxious fumes of rum and Coke clouded the space around us. I hadn't flushed the toilet, or so he said. *Yellow water.* I said I thought I had, but if I hadn't, I was sorry. I was tired, I had a test in Washington state history the next day, and could I go to bed?

"Do you think it's funny?" he slurred. A fist—surprisingly fast, considering the difficulty he'd been having just standing upright—shot from his side and into my face, sending me twirling, spinning to the floor.

It might have been a beautifully acrobatic maneuver, slightly funny if it hadn't hurt so badly. With everything to run from and nowhere to run to, I hid behind the holly bush that shielded our dining-room window from that of the Perkins's next door.

* * *

"I think I see it, Papa." My son pushed past me and crawled deeper into the underbrush. Scraping away the layer of dead leaves that was the thorny carpet beneath us, he uncovered an egg-shaped rock. "Darn," he said. "I thought it was a baseball."

"It's all right," I told him. "It's in here somewhere; we'll find it."

* * *

"Warren?" My mother's voice had called, shaky and pleading. "Are you there? It's okay to come in." Lenny had gone to bed, done with all of it. My mother met me at the door, her cheek puffed and darkening, an empty space where a front tooth should have been. "It's going to be fine."

He was gone for a couple days after that, sent away by Mom. No man was going to hit her; she'd said this many times before and I believed her. But Lenny was like a tenacious rat, chased out but somehow squeezing his bedraggled body back into the house, and this time was no different. My mother and he had worked something out, had some private conversation of which I was to be no part. As far as anyone else was concerned, my mother had been in a car accident. I'd gotten hit in the mouth by a baseball, a wild overthrow during an otherwise innocent game of catch. Clearly, nothing had happened.

In this family, I was reminded, nothing *ever* happens.

CHAPTER 3

Wнем I was young, prepubescent, there was no doubt that I looked like my mother. Strangers would remark as we walked into the room, "Oh, I can see he's your son." The same fullness of the face, the pale blue eyes, the thickness and light brown shading of our hair gave us away in an instant. Physical traits of movement had also carried over, if only by habit. When my mother walked she favored her right side slightly; an earlier injury had caused a tiny difference in the lengths of her legs. Curiously, I had also developed this gait, a small tilt to one side as I walked, and I'd grown accustomed to people asking me if I'd hurt myself.

But as time went on, shades of my father began to creep through. Snapshots taken at certain angles highlight the shape of my nose, the slightness of my chin. My half-cocked grin and gentle tilt of the head accentuate the fact that, like it or not, I am my father's son, and when I hear my mother gasp and see her look guiltily away for having done so, I know that she sees it too. Visits to the barbershop would end with a carpet of hair that was increasingly white and as I neared my fortieth birthday, I found myself torn between feelings of desperation and satisfied resolve for having predicted things so correctly. "By the time I'm forty," I'd begun saying as the first gray strands appeared on my twenty-year-old head, "my hair will be completely white." My mother had begun dying her hair at nineteen and her father had been completely gray by his fourth decade. I accepted it then and I accept it now, just as I've come to terms with my chin, my nose, the shape of my head. That's the thing about DNA: gifts handed down are given outside one's control. Short of surgery and chemicals, we are more or less forced to grow within the confines of what nature has mapped for us.

Still, there are moments as I pass my reflection in a storefront window, as I stare back at myself from the mirror while running the razor along the line of my beard, that I fight the twinge of self-loathing shooting through me. A slight movement of the head, a forced furrow of the brow—anything to chase away the image of my father looking back at me.

When asked where they see themselves as grown-ups, my young sons often speak with uncertain hesitation. The idea of being an adult, of shouldering the responsibilities of manhood, of parenthood, is so far removed from the everyday tasks they face as rambunctious boys that the concept is completely foreign to them. I can empathize. As a young boy, I struggled with the image of myself as the adult, the parent, the man. I'd never pictured myself as a copy of either of my parents, neither in appearance nor profession. Most of the time, I'd see myself as a cross between Mike Brady, patriarch of *The Brady Bunch,* and the dad from *The Courtship of Eddie's Father.* I'd have dark hair, chiseled features, a forest green split-level house, and infinite patience and humor with my children. I still strive for that—the patience part, that is. It's hard to be a patient parent to three active boys. I'm long over the desire for a split-level and the rest is beyond hope. The typical stresses of everyday life—work, time, and unmet goals—too often incite me to act on raw impulses rather than foresight and I sometimes find it easier to snap an intimidating retort than to think ahead and construct a thoughtful, proactive response. My sons' energy, tenaciousness, and drive for natural discovery challenge me as a parent more often than I'm comfortable admitting; after all, I'm a schoolteacher and in the classroom I'm a model of control and reason. So I find it mysterious and ironic that when my youngest son throws a tantrum over an issue I find ridiculous, I might react by stomping toward him, my teeth and hands clenched, my eyes blazing. It's during those moments that I am my father, and this terrifies me. I force my hands to my sides and when I have the impulse to throw a curt comment, to shame my son into behaving more appropriately, I am my stepfather and that disgusts me beyond imagination. I bite my tongue, take a breath, and try with all my soul to help my child learn without fear. It's these inherited traits, these toxic hand-me-downs planted in me that I know I must control and shape; I must break the pattern that has been set before me.

It seems like I've forever sought to redefine myself behind the shadows of the men who have tried to raise me. For most of my life, I've been able to do this with relative ease; simply step outside of the path ahead of me. Wearing a hardhat, dragging on a Marlboro, laying pipe, or running a saw never much appealed to me in my youth and that was fine for the most part. It kept me a safe distance from the less-than-healthy men in my life and allowed me the chance to imagine my own adulthood as a completely open plain.

So what happens when a man finds himself planted in the role in which the only models he has ever had are men whose influence he has spent his whole life trying to escape? It's not enough to simply say, "I'll do the opposite of what they did." My son, rescued from the emptiness of an orphanage, is counting on me to be all that I'd ever wished for in a father and I'm discovering that it's not so easy to simply "do the opposite" of what has been done to me. It's horrifying to own, but the spores of my forefathers are in the soil that feeds me, like a dormant fungus lying in wait, and they keep appearing, breaking through in spite of what my heart and my memory are telling me.

So what do I do? Bury my father and stepfather and all that they represent completely? Pick and choose through my memories, taking only the scenes that don't cause my stomach to tighten with anxiety? Try to construct a version of the ideal father like a Frankenstein's monster, a false creation pieced together from vignettes of clumsy parenting?

The problem with that theory is that those segments are parts of me. They *are* me. I can't select from the things I own, and it's a painful thing to accept that. The best I can do is work to understand those poisons that are there, and only then can I seek to control them.

If only it were that easy.

CHAPTER 4

I'VE NEVER BEEN COMPLETELY HAPPY with the garden plot I inherited along with our house. There are parts of it that have worked for me; I've always liked the purple puffballs of the chives in late June. A few color combinations have given me pleasure when I've mean-

dered through the paths; the surprise of gray-stemmed poppies, springing up from between the clumps of sage, rose-hued sedums spilling out
from a backdrop of deep green currant bushes are always a warming
sight even on the gloomiest of Seattle days. But overall, I've come to feel
like the steward of a needy miniature world with which I've had neither
a substantial connection nor any real affinity: forced responsibility without real acceptance.

My partner Shayne and I bought the property in the spring of 2001.
Although the land had actually been harvested of its old-growth trees by
a lumber company decades earlier, the previous owners took what had
been, for them, an untouched parcel of land, and carved the landscape as
they had envisioned their own private universe. The acreage once again
was thick with lush ferns, huckleberry bushes, and towering evergreens.
They built a small house and a few useful outbuildings, and commenced
to create pockets of gardens throughout the five-acre piece. We were en-
chanted by the place at our first viewing.

Shayne, a landscape designer, eagerly embraced the ornamental gardens and I was "gifted" with the vegetable garden, the one collection of
plantings that we felt I could handle without ruining, to take on as my
very own. The rigid rows of onions, beans, and various leafy edibles outlined the garden like a map, sandy paths crisscrossing in a reliably familiar grid. Here and there a perennial popped up—delphiniums, black-
eyed Susans, and irises of several colors drew the eye over the tops of the
salad-fixings. For the first season, everything was wonderful. Our salad
bowls were full, the mulch dutifully spread by the previous owners did
its job, and I moved into autumn loving the garden I now called my own.

An experienced gardener would have known what to expect in the
coming season, but I was a novice. This was all new to me. Months went
by, things died back, others awoke. Dandelions I'd pulled weeks earlier
seemed to suddenly regenerate, poking from the soil to tantalize me with
their bright yellow heads before exploding into a thousand tiny skydiv-
ing seeds. Forget-me-nots I'd gazed over lovingly last season now ran
rampant, filling the beds that were supposed to be coming up cabbages.
Another detail I'd yet to learn: vegetables are not perennial. They must
be planted *every* season. The *Northwest Gardener's Guide* pushed me even

further—apparently I was expected to sow new seeds *each month*, to ensure a year-round vegetable medley.

I worked in the preformed beds, occasionally trying seeds and starts, half-heartedly harvesting arugula, chard, mustard greens, and several varieties of radishes, each spicier than the next. I pulled weeds, and the muscles of my lower back. I raked my arms on wild blackberry vines and welted my face on clandestine nettle plantlets hiding under the gooseberry bushes. Season upon season, I hopelessly functioned as the begrudging caretaker of this white elephant that was my garden. The areas left unattended were, to the many invasive species waiting in the wings, an absolute dream. Tiny green worms infested the gooseberries and, in spite of pruning the bushes nearly to the dirt each year, the little guys showed up reliably every spring like an unwanted relative. The few plants with which I'd begun to have an affinity were quickly devoured by hordes of slugs. Before long, the weeds outnumbered the vegetables and the only things left were fennel and lavender and the various roses that the automatic sprinklers could reach. I was done.

The reality was that I'd had neither the interest nor the drive to address my garden with any level of enthusiasm. After all, it was a thing—however potentially beautiful—not of my own creation. I'd inherited it and perhaps within that mere fact sprung my bitterness and stubborn resolve. I'd had no control, no ownership of what grew in there, just the responsibility to keep it going regardless of what filled in the borders and what lay hidden under the branches. Pests, noxious weeds, dead foliage.

I'd become convinced that I was stuck with what was already there. After all, I had neither the knowledge nor the skills to substitute or change any part of it. This collection of flora and the three hundred square feet of soil on which it existed was mine and I'd always believed that if I intended for life to continue upon that same square, I would have to walk its rows and work within the frames I had been given.

My garden, with its excruciating constrictions and unyielding frustrations, had become a reflection of my life. I'd felt trapped by the branches of the family tree that loomed massive over my head. In my mind it formed an immovable canopy blocking even the tiniest slivers of light. Alcoholism, violence, and dysfunction of the worst kind formed the roots that were my culture, shaping my very essence, and they were hidden far below the surface, too deep to even consider. I had my mother's eyes, my father's nerves, and all the baggage that came along with the genes that transferred those traits to me. In a sense, I was stuck.

But not completely.

It was a late summer Saturday, early enough in the day to escape the heat of a high sun but late enough to avoid angering the neighbors with the roar of the motor. I dragged the rototiller across the driveway and up the center of the garden, right next to where the spinach and clover had been just weeks before, and I wondered: *How long will it take me to tear up three hundred square feet of weedy ground?* No matter. Gripping the handle, I planted my feet firmly in the dirt and pulled the cord.

CHAPTER 5

"WHAT DO YOU WANT TO GO DIGGIN' THERE FOR?" he'd asked. "Drunks, thieves, and jailbirds. That's all you'll find." Famously, my mother's great-uncle George had announced this to his daughter Valoyce when she expressed an interest in our family tree. She'd told this to my mother and, some years later, my mother told me.

"I don't know what you expect to find," she'd said when I brought up the subject of a genealogical search. "But I guess I'm a little curious, too."

Uncle George's words made no difference to me, really. After all, I'd seen plenty of vices in my lifetime, right on my own branch of the family tree. Alcoholism, petty theft, trials, and convictions had each made regular appearances in my family since I could remember. What stories could I possibly find in my lineage that would be more scandalous than those that existed in my own memories? I was hungry for information and eager to start looking. So, in spite of Uncle George's warning, I pushed ahead without hesitation.

*   *   *

Renovating a garden can't be done impulsively. I've learned that it takes planning and foresight—an understanding of where the garden stands and a vision of where it will be. Before ripping up the soil, I'd lifted the plants I'd planned to keep in my new garden—the roses, herbs, and currants—and carefully set them aside, safe from the churning blades of the tiller. A meticulous line of fluorescent-orange spray paint snaked through the square, a template I'd drawn for the path I envisioned winding through a cutting garden of color, scents, and excited bees. I wanted real change, a move from rigid predictability to a feeling of brightness and visual nourishment.

I like the warmth of a big bouquet. I get a far greater burst of pleasure gathering sunflowers, delphiniums, and lavender sprigs than I could ever get from cabbages and carrots. Even as a child, I recognized the joy that a fistful of flowers could bring. Flowers then were gifts of opportunity. Wildflowers gathered in the meadows across the road from my maternal grandmother's house and stuffed into the neck of one of my grand-father's beer bottles never failed to bring squeals of glee from her, and she'd tell us the story of her father's funeral once again.

"The shops were all closed to honor him; it was like a parade, all down Main Street," she'd say, her lips bent in a proud grin at the memory of her daddy, a revered county prosecutor. "There were so many flowers at his office and the house, you'd think there wasn't a single bloom left atop a stem in all of Mississippi."

As an adult, though, fresh flowers became a luxury, gifts bought from a flower shop with my hard-earned money for the benefit of others. The florist would craft a clutch of daisies or carnations for a Mother's Day bouquet or throw together a generic arrangement to send to an acquaintance's funeral. Now, flowers were no longer picked, they were purchased. The simple truth was, I wanted to pick flowers again.

* * *

I stood in the open space of my newly turned garden, my boots sinking in the soft black soil, my gloves gripping the rake as I pulled it through the till. I paused every few yards to turn the rake head upward and pick out the snags of roots and weeds that had found their way into the teeth.

Dandelion taproots and starts of unwanted brush went into the wheelbarrow, and the gentle singsong of my youngest son Dmitry's voice drifted from the sand pile, in cadence with the scratching of his tiny shovel and my ancient rake. It was a nursery rhyme, I'm sure, though I can't recall exactly which one. There were a half-dozen or so in his repertoire. I'd picked up the verse with him, like I usually did, and he'd turned to look at me, smiling as the two of us finished with dramatic flair.

And the irony of it all washed over me with the sound of the nursery rhyme, just as clear, just as simple as the melody of that silly song. I was a father to a son of my own, like Mr. Brady and Mr. Eddie's Father, and my responsibility to him was something I could not wander through blindly, like I had my garden, figuring it out along the way and hoping that I would discover the right path. I was at a place of opportunity. My son didn't fear me, didn't take pains to avoid me. The patterns we were beginning to create were good; small rituals that made us laugh and look forward to doing it all again.

Our children are born as clean slates, it is said, but that's not true at all. Genetics mark us with a map already in place. A packet of seeds I put into the dirt is pretty predictable, as long as I do what's required to raise the plant to adulthood. But climate, nutrients, pests—all can affect the plant's life. Our family, the crucial people in our lives, are like gardeners, nurturing us through the seasons, influencing us with their actions, their habits, their words. Our son came to us when he was nearly eighteen months old; his life had already begun in earnest, so it was our task as his new parents to shepherd him the rest of the way. His genetic slate may have been already in place, but his journey was and is far from complete. For that matter, so is mine.

I realized then that if I wanted to ensure an optimal environment for my child, to completely move outside the patterns of dysfunction that continued to creep up in my life, I would need to get to a place where I understood—truly understood—the unhealthy foliage that filled my own family tree. And to do this, to grasp the origins of my flashes of anger, the discomfort of seeing and hearing my last name used in conjunction with my first, the minor recoil I did when black-and-white family photos showed resemblances to my father that were undeniable, I would need to begin clearing the soil from the roots of my family tree, scraping away at the dirt and detritus to see what was really there. Looking at the branches would give me some names and a few facts; this I knew. To get at the heart of my family—the essential elements of *me*— I would have to dig as well, to uncover the roots hidden deep beneath the surface.

The more we dig, of course, the more we uncover. I can still see an image of my seven-year-old self with a neighbor pal; we are using my mother's tarnished serving spoon to excavate the remains of an old home site in the woods behind our house. The promise of buried treasure is exhilarating and even the end result, an old pint whiskey bottle, can't quench our rabid curiosity. I found myself pulled to the treasure hunt of genealogy, the search for the ancient footprints of my family, in the same way. The very notion of finding something precious, some amazing fact that might redeem my ominous memories, was a call that grew louder the more I tried to quash it. I really wanted something good, something of which to be proud. But the path that appeared in front of me, sometimes bright, often nearly indiscernible, was one over which I had no control. A turn here, a dead end there, the trail would continue meanderingly until one night a startling, horrific find—one from which there would be no turning back.

CHAPTER 6

A FINE STRETCH OF SUMMER DAYS moved into the drizzly early dusk that is the trademark of the Pacific Northwest and I found myself finally able to settle in and devote more time to genealogical research. Night after night I sat at the computer, following one lead into another, collecting intriguing bits of identifying information on my parents' various ancestors. The fact that there were people out there in the world, individuals whom I would never meet who were connected to me by some distant, far-reaching twig of the family tree was mind-boggling. They'd already laid the groundwork for me, recording names, dates, and birthplaces; I could take what I learned from one source and connect it to another found resource. It was giant jigsaw puzzle, the edges forming a frame and the interior just beginning to come into view. And then suddenly, after weeks of deciphering the great arching familial maps that had been created and posted on Web sites for all to see, I'd stumbled upon the final piece to the puzzle that, up to then, had perplexed me to no end. Old Uncle George had not been kidding.

While the search for my father's side of the family had been going swimmingly (forefathers in Wales, a surprise Jewish ancestor, an owner of a sugar plantation), my mother's side had proven to be frustratingly vacant. I found a bit about my mother's maternal side, a maiden name here and there, and that was all. It baffled me. With a family name like Dondino, how could there *not* be usable results? There were Dondinos living in Italy, but I knew they were not my Dondinos. After weeks of futile searching, I'd assumed I was finished and that what little I'd found was all there was to be found.

Some weeks later I was browsing at the newsstand, killing time between errands, and I picked up an issue of a computer tech magazine. I'm not a tech-savvy kind of person, but a blurb on the cover about genealogical searches caught my attention. The article inside listed a half-dozen search engines that I hadn't yet tried. When I got home that night, I decided I would try to find my mother's family once more, see if in fact these additional tools would work where the other ones hadn't. I wasn't optimistic. I sat down at the computer and put the list of search engines in front of me. Fingers on the home row, I entered the first URL and pecked away at the familiar search terms, Dondino and Minnesota. Within seconds, a heading I hadn't seen before popped up and the subtext was stunning. There was something about a rape, references to a lynching—and it had taken place in Duluth. An ominous feeling crept over me as I clicked on the link and began to read, scanning warily, baffled over where my family's name would appear.

As I stared at the monitor, horrified, eyes burning and gut slowly knotting, the growing clarity of truth began to sink in. I scrolled down the text haltingly, my hands shaking. The link had led me to the June 7, 2000, issue of the *Ripsaw News,* a weekly news and entertainment newspaper in Duluth, Minnesota. The article was titled "Duluth's Lingering Shame" and in it, writer Heidi Bakk-Hansen chronicled the night of June 15, 1920, when six black circus workers had been arrested in connection with the alleged rape of a white teenaged girl, accused by the girl and her boyfriend. Within hours, a mob of somewhere between five and ten thousand townspeople clamored around the Duluth city jail demanding vigilante justice. In the end, three of the six men hung dead from a nearby lamppost and a community struggled to come to grips with the awful truth that, once the facts reached the light of day, no assault had actually happened. The men had been innocent; the girl and her boyfriend had been lying.

As I read through the article, my initial excitement over discovering new information turned to trepidation and then dread as I began to realize that I was about to find something that might very well change everything I thought I knew about my family. About two-thirds of the way through the article, I came across a name that up until then I'd have given anything to find. Now, I was hoping it was somebody else.

Few members of the lynch mob received any punishment. Two who did stand trial, Henry Stephenson and Louis Dondino, served less than half of their five-year sentences for rioting.

My mind was spinning, not just at the news with which I'd suddenly been hit, but with the realization that I would very soon be forced to share this unthinkable story with my mother. That up until that moment I'd subscribed to an idealized view of my great-grandfather. To my mother, her grandfather had been a figure of warmth, of unconditional love. He was her hero. To me, he had been all of these things, too, but only because I'd heard the adoration in her voice and seen the longing in her eyes each time she'd spoken of him. The only concrete relationship I had with him was rooted in a few old photos and a singular memento that had been passed from him to me.

My grandfather had given me an old Hohner harmonica when I was about nine years old. It had come in a tidy black case with purple velvet lining, and on the side of the instrument was a small knob that, when pulled, changed the key a half step. I had little idea how to play it but I found that by rolling it slowly back and forth across my lips, moderating my breath in and out, pulling and pushing the knob, I could make sounds that were beautifully haunting to my young ears. It had a musty, delicious smell and when I wasn't making music, I'd bring it down to the carpet among my Hot Wheels and pretend it was a shiny silver ferry boat, sailing sleekly through the blue pile carpeting.

The harmonica had belonged to my grandpa's father, a man I knew as my great-grandpa Louis. My mother called him Pa. He'd died well before I was born, when my mother had been just a teenager. I used to imagine my great-grandpa Louis playing his harmonica as he danced in his kitchen—there had been a photo of him holding something up near his mouth that my young mind had always interpreted as the harmonica (I'd discover later, upon closer inspection, that the harmonica was in fact a pint bottle). Still, he'd lived on in my memory as a man to be loved and admired, a gentle soul who'd helped soften the jagged, rough edges of my mother's young life. In photos, I can see that like the harmonica his hair is silver, like his son's, his granddaughter's and now, his great-grandson's.

My own images of my great-grandfather had always been filtered through my mother and now, suddenly, I had a new picture of him coming at me through a journalist's pen. It was my mother's stories, her memories forced through the perspective of an adoring twelve-year-old girl that had created the man I'd known as Louis Dondino. Her wistful narrative combined the grinding organ melodies and thrill-drenched screams echoing from the carnival as she stood anxiously in the doorway waiting for her beloved grandfather to come, to take her from her drab house to the carnival, where the real excitement was. She told me how her fingers gripped the edge of the screen door, holding tightly to keep it still and quiet. It moved slightly against the weight of her body and a deep, smoky squeak echoed from the rusty hinges through the kitchen and into the living room, catching the attention of her mother, my grandmother Margaret.

"Nellie Rose, close that door or there'll be more flies inside than out," her mother had scolded. She'd always called her daughter by her first and middle names, a trait that she'd brought with her all the way from Gulfport, Mississippi, to their home in Edmonds, Washington. "He'll be here when he gets here."

It was Labor Day weekend and that meant the carnival was up and running on the campus of Edmonds High School, a few blocks from my mother's home just north of the downtown core. It also meant that her grandpa Louis would be there to take his only granddaughter to the show. Sister, he called her affectionately, and she called him Pa. He was my mother's savior and she was the apple of his eye. "This little girl is tough as nails," he'd brag to his buddies at the Sail Inn Tavern. "She can shoot the neck off a beer bottle at forty paces." And she could, too; first with a BB gun, then with the gift her daddy had gotten her on her tenth Christmas, a .22 rifle.

*   *   *

My mother would have no way of knowing it then, but she stood directly in the center of a tense, recurring battle between my grandpa Ray—her father—and her own grandfather. My great-grandfather Louis had been in the habit of spoiling his granddaughter as much as he could, and this fanned the flames of jealousy and paternal competition in his son Ray something fierce. My mother could never understand the explosive anger and disrespect her father showed to his own pa, the gentle old man whom everyone else in her life seemed to absolutely love. Insight would come in bits and pieces, usually in beer-infused diatribes from her father that were meant for both everyone and no one in particular. The emerging truth was that Ray could never reconcile how a man who had been so neglectful during his son's upbringing could dare to present himself as a beacon of parental mores. Where had this jovial old man been thirty years earlier when his own boy needed a father, on those long evenings Ray spent on his knees scrubbing the orphanage floors and the early mornings in the sanctuary, forced to kneel in empty prayer?

"Get off your ass and do some work around here for a change," my grandpa Ray would growl at his daughter whenever she'd return from doing some odd jobs for his dad. "I don't understand why you got all this time and energy to do chores for that old man and not for me." And there had been something more, something unspoken in the Dondino home.

21

Even as a child, my mother could sense that there was something "really, really bad between Daddy and Pa," though it never seemed to come to light.

*   *   *

She'd grown impatient, my mother who was that little girl, waiting for her Pa to take her to the carnival, for the sleepover afterwards on his wonderful, lumpy old sofa. She began to pace and complain, but a rattling sound caught her ear. She swung open the screen door to see her old Pa ambling up the alley, trudging behind his homemade wooden cart, his mutts Spotty and Teddy perched obediently inside. Alongside the dogs was her Pa's shiny knotty cane, the one he'd made himself from the branch of an aged cherry tree. An old leg injury had made the cane his constant companion. My mother dashed back inside the house to gather her blankets for a sleepover with her grandpa, slamming the door shut.

"Now don't be fillin' up on candy and sodas," my grandmother warned her daughter as she watched her pile blankets into the cart and scratch the rough fur behind the dogs' ears.

"Oh now, Margaret," Louis reassured his daughter-in-law, "it's once a year."

"And you," she said, drying her hands on her apron and shooting a stern look at Louis, "don't let me hear news that you took her gamblin' again." The previous year, Louis had shown my mother the mouse race at the arcade. The two of them had laid a bet on which color hole the mouse would run through when it was released. When my mother guessed correctly and came home with a pocket full of dimes, my grandmother was furious. Gambling in any form was a nonnegotiable for her. Her strict Southern Baptist teachings had forbidden dice or even a deck of cards in her house, a rule that would last until her dying day. When I stayed at my grandparents' home years later I spent many tedious hours tearing paper into fifty-two scraps to create a playing deck of my own or labeling rocks with numbers for a decent roll of the dice. "Don't worry, Margaret," Louis assured my grandmother calmly. "I'll be good."

My mother grabbed on to her grandpa's arm as they made their way to his tiny house, up the street toward town, just behind Brownie's Café.

Louis drew his hand from his pocket and reached toward his grand-daughter. "Here ya go, sister," he said. "You'll need some spending change for the carnival." Wisps of white hair lifted from the sides and top of his balding head; the characteristic crevasses that lined his forehead and formed bookends for his eyes deepened as his smile widened.

"I got my own, Pa," she said proudly, beaming up at him. My mother had brought the change collected from days of combing the neighborhood for bottles. Beer bottles were worth a penny each then, sometimes a few extra cents if she'd kept them all neatly in the case. Quart beer bottles were more, three cents each, standard pop bottles were two cents, and a quart pop bottle was the big cash cow at a nickel each. She'd typically collect several cases of Rainier bottles from her own home, though her parents would only allow her to take a couple cases at a time so that people wouldn't know how much her father actually drank (as if it would have been any kind of mystery in a small town like Edmonds). She also knew which other homes in the neighborhood were known to accumulate bottles and she'd wheel her booty to the back door of the Sail Inn Tavern and bang loudly, waiting for someone to come and open it. After inspecting her bottles ("You clean these out real good? I don't want old beer stinkin' up the place.") the owner would pay her and she'd be on her way, briefly thankful for her father's addiction.

Where her father was volatile, her Pa was gentle. Pa was good, where Daddy was bitter and angry. Pa was the calm in Nellie Rose's otherwise unforgiving life and in his home she was safe and warm. In his house there was no need to worry about being awakened in the middle of the night by a drunken scene, her father cursing God and his mortal hucksters, spitting hatred and contempt for painful boyhood moments, while her mother loudly whispered pleas for forgiveness to her husband, "Please, Ray, lord have mercy it's in the past, you gotta stop, Ray, just stop."

In my mother's memory, it's been a wonderfully exhausting day at the carnival; she feels a quiet sense of peace, nestled in the warmth of woolen blankets and the slight glow of the streetlamp outside her grandpa's living room. It is well past midnight, beyond the cliffhangers of the weekend radio serials, *Dragnet* and *Mr. District Attorney,* when her eyelids began to flutter at last, drooping heavily. The ominous music for the next episode of *The Shadow* swells from the cloth-covered speakers, a slight crackle in the background of the chilling narration, and she drifts off to sleep knowing that for this moment, all in her little world is perfect.

CHAPTER 7

FAMILY TREES, CENSUS DATA, anecdotal tales, and even photographs can give a person a rudimentary, one-sided view of his or her family. Dates, names, and trivia begin to fill in the puzzle. A picture posed and taken under the best of light with the subject carefully still will capture a moment in time, often when things are at their best and most presentable. Like a thousand-piece jigsaw puzzle, the completed image can be detailed and colorful, but sadly lacking any real depth.

When I discovered the *Ripsaw News* article I began to collect the complex pieces of history that would help me form the outline of my own complicated puzzle. With those bits of data would come a flood of questions about my great-grandfather, the young Louis Dondino. What kind of life had he made for his son? What about the community he lived in? What was Duluth like in the early twentieth century? How did African Americans fare in this northern city nearly fifty years after emancipation?

Context can explain an action, but seldom does it excuse. I've always maintained this—with myself, my children, my students. Still, I knew I would have to seek my explanations with the hope that they would help provide an understanding I so desperately needed. Only when one truly understands the whole picture of an action, I feel, can one begin to take responsibility for it. To understand the context of that night in June of 1920 I would need to reconstruct the life of my great-grandfather, and my grandfather, as vividly as possible. As in my garden, before I could even consider tilling the soil to reform the landscape, I would need to educate myself and truly understand what had come before me in order to create the pathways that would be there after.

Before I discovered the *Ripsaw News* article I'd known a few basic facts about my great-grandfather's younger days. His wife had died when his son, my grandfather Ray, was a young boy and Louis had raised him with occasional help from his own parents. His parents lived on a farm. Louis worked as a logger; oftentimes his son, Ray, was forced to live in a Catholic orphanage. There was intense anger and bitterness between the two men that lasted until both of their deaths. That was about all I knew: a few clues and a lot of empty space. I did the math in order to create a readable timeline, studied the geography to gain a sense of place, and painstakingly scoured the history. Over time, I was able to pull together a reasonable life's portrait of the man who would come to be a beloved patriarch to one family, a vilified mob leader to countless others. And with this portrait, the emptiness shrank and the understanding grew.

*   *   *

By 1920, my great-grandfather Louis had lived in the Great Lakes area nearly all of his thirty-eight years. Born in Meade, Michigan (a town I've not been able to find any mention of today), in 1882, he was the second of six children, his only sister being the eldest. His father and mother, William and Sarah, emigrated from Ontario to Michigan in 1860 when they were both sixteen, settling the area to farm.

It's a common assumption that the Dondino lineage was Italian, given the spelling of the name. However, Louis's parents did not speak or write English, and the story goes that when they told an immigration official their last name was Dondineau, the impatient and ill-informed clerk wrote it as Dondino. To this day, there are Dondinos and Dondineaus throughout the Great Lakes region whose ancestry is very likely linked somehow. To further confuse the matter, records of enlisted men in William's Civil War division show his name as Dandenon, Dondeno, and, as it is on his headstone, Dandenow. As in a lot of genealogy research, the variations in spelling are frustratingly difficult to differentiate.

William and Sarah moved with their infant son, Louis, and his older sister from Meade to Duluth, Minnesota, in 1882. The 1880s had been a booming time for the port city, especially in the production of lumber and lumber products. Thanks to the railroads and shipping routes through Lake Superior connecting Duluth commercially to the markets of Chicago, Cleveland, and the great Atlantic coast cities, by 1884, Duluth mills would operate at a capacity of thirty million board feet of lumber annually. Elevators, lumber warehouses, and expansive docks had been built to accommodate the growing industry, and the population of Duluth had grown right along with it. From 1880 to 1890, Duluth's population would rise from about seven thousand to nearly forty thousand. The Dondinos's arrival in Duluth in 1882 coincided with a severe typhoid epidemic that was ravaging the city. St. Luke's Hospital, the first in Duluth, had just opened its doors above a blacksmith's shop for the sole purpose of tackling the outbreak. For my ancestors and countless others, the future was both a promise and a terrifying prospect. Fortune could be had just as easily as death.

*　　*　　*

It hadn't been the discovery of the lynching that had surprised me. The concept was certainly not foreign to me. My grandmother Margaret had been born and raised in Mississippi; growing up, I'd been all too aware of the realities of violent racism that had been part of the culture of her own young life. Westerns on Saturday-afternoon television often showed a lynching or two, a portrayal of earned justice for horse thieving or stagecoach robbing. But the idea that a mob lynching could have happened in the north, far from the KKK rallies and cross-burnings of the Deep South, still seemed like an anomaly. It wasn't, though, as I would discover over and over again. In early American culture, lynchings had been a form of vigilantism practiced throughout the land, regardless of the condemned man's (or woman's) race.

In late April of 1882, the same year that my great-grandfather settled in Duluth with his parents, a twenty-five-year-old Irish metalworker was arrested in Minneapolis, just a day's trip by rail from the Dondinos's new home. Frank McManus had moved to the City of Lakes five years previously, having spent much of his adult life working in the iron mills of Boston. Upon his arrest, McManus was taken to the Minneapolis city jail and hidden away securely—for good reason. Police speculated that when word got out that this man had brutally raped the four-year-old daughter of J. P. Spear, a local tin-manufacturing worker, there was likely to be trouble. And sure enough, by two the next morning, it showed up at the jail—sixty men strong.

The mob forced their way in, using a large timber as a battering ram, and demanded the sheriff lead them to the prisoner. The sheriff refused, but a frightened night watchman directed them to cell number three, on the upper tier of the jailhouse. McManus was quickly found; the mob swarmed over him, cuffed his wrists, and took him to the Spear home for positive identification. While her daughter lay dying in the next room, Mrs. Spear shook, glaring at the shackled McManus. "It is the man," she cried. "Take him away."

The men led McManus from the Spear home to a bare oak tree, carefully arranged the noose around his neck, and asked him if he had anything to say. McManus continued to proclaim his innocence, identifying himself as one Tim Crowley, son of Nancy Ann Crowley of South Boston. He whispered a message to one of the vigilantes that was to be delivered to his mother before finally confessing to the rape, with the rationale that he had been drunk when he'd assaulted the little girl. With nothing left to be said, the men tied McManus's hands behind his back and he was "swung off."

A photograph of the lynching was taken and issued as a postcard (not unusual at the time), perhaps as a warning to other men who might contemplate such an act. In the photo, the mob of hundreds, wearing hats and dressed in suits and ties, dominate the black-and-white image. If not for the solitary figure dangling from a branch (he almost looks as though he's standing on the shoulders of the crowd) it could be a group of revelers posing at a parade or a sporting event. Hands folded or planted firmly on hips; broad, satisfied grins; all before the backdrop of the quaint, ghostly glow of a farmhouse fronted with a dark stripe of death.

It's difficult to imagine what my great-great-grandfather William and his family would have thought about this act of vigilantism; I like to imagine that they'd have been mortified, or at least troubled. In all likelihood, though, the Dondinos probably shrugged it off as a fitting consequence for the crime. "A woman's virtue is above all else" was a message passed from parent to child in my family, all the way down to my own mother's ears. "You can spit and curse, but it's no kind of man that would hurt a woman."

*　　*　　*

My great-great-grandfather William Dondineau began working in one of the several mills that lined the edge of Lake Superior, fitting comfortably into the white working-class immigrant population of Duluth's West End. Industry was growing and William did his best to keep up with it, staying in the lumber and logging trade for the next ten years. Eventually his advancing age and memories of his earlier farming days drew him away from the city, and in 1896 William and Sarah pulled their children from school (Louis was now fourteen years old and in the fourth grade) and settled near Superior, Wisconsin, on a small homestead in the tiny farming town of Bennett.

The photos we have of early Bennett show a series of small homesteads, often surrounded by peeled and cut logs stacked in triangular formation, waiting for transport to the mills. The land surrounding the half-dozen or so farmhouses is bare and open; if the notations on the backs of the pictures didn't identify the location specifically, it would be easy to mistake it for a Midwestern Plains town. Modest farmhouses and smaller tarpaper shacks are connected by wooden boardwalk-like sidewalks to what passes as a well-traveled Main Street.

My great-grandfather Louis stayed on the homestead with his siblings to help run the small farm and tend to his parents in their old age. In about 1904, at the age of twenty-two, Louis married a young Dutchwoman, Nellie Vanderpool, and in 1907 my grandfather Ray was born. Six years later, Nellie would die of an unknown illness. Louis left Bennett a widower and single father, returning across the waters of Lake Superior to raise his son in the now booming city of Duluth.

CHAPTER 8

Like his father, my grandfather worked in the sawmills, as did his father before him. The timber trade spread from Minnesota to Washington State and the Dondinos followed. The men in my family were loggers and sawmill workers, embedded in the grain of the lumber industry. Among the family portraits and backyard snapshots scattered in a shoebox of old photos are several pictures of my forefathers standing proudly in front of enormous felled logs, saws or axes in hand, plaid shirts tucked firmly into rugged jeans. For four generations, the men in my family have worked hard to provide for their families, clearing the natural landscape of its towering timber in the process, cutting the fallen corpses into neat boards that would one day be used to create a framework for the new homes of happy families everywhere.

When my own parents met in Edmonds, Washington, in July 1965, their future family was already nearly complete. My mother came to the marriage with my sister Karen in tow, a two-year-old who had been born out of wedlock (a crime worthy of ostracizing in 1962; Karen would forever be the living embodiment of Don't Ever Think It Can't Happen the First Time). My father arrived at his second marriage with his own children as well: Julie, also age two; Brad, age four; and Beth, age five. The two single parents had been introduced by a well-meaning, albeit shortsighted, friend. My mother desperately needed new tires for her car; my father worked at a service station and knew how to use a lug wrench. And maybe the coupling, if not perfect, was at least deemed socially acceptable for each of them.

In hindsight, I can see that their union might have been driven more by their desire for stability than by chemistry or any real emotional connection. I don't remember witnessing a great deal of conflict between my mother and father, really, but those moments of gentle affection, shared laughter, the joy in one another's company that a child sees here and there when his parents are in love—those things just weren't there for me to see. And when I speak with my mother about it today, it becomes uncomfortably clear that, at least in her eyes, they were together simply because they were there for each other.

"It was 1965 and I was an unwed mother in a small town," she explains. "That wasn't okay then." Hearing my mother describe her ostracism is heartbreaking to me today. But people who had been friends to my grandmother for years, women who had accepted recipes and prayers and heartfelt good wishes from her, walked past without so much as a glance, ignoring her as if she'd been a complete stranger.

"It was hard to see her go through that and it upsets me even today," my mother goes on. "Anyway, your dad was a nice guy, we got along well and he had a stable job. He definitely understood the need to be a responsible parent. I think we were what the other one needed at the time." They settled about thirty miles north of Seattle in the Boeing and Weyerhaeuser suburb of Everett. Almost a year after they married, I came to join this colorful and raucous bunch.

For as long as I can remember, my father worked the lumber mills. The vernacular of the sawmills had become such a part of me that for a time I believed I was destined to do the same. I imagined myself like him, leaving the house before my kids came home from school, returning home well past the hour they'd been tucked into bed. Sawdust-caked boots, soft yellow earplugs, and a nagging, sore back would be the future I had to look forward to.

One of my earliest memories of my father is of him coming out of his shift at the Simpson Lee mill. I'm young, maybe four, and it's one of the rare occasions when it's still daylight by the time he's finished his shift. My mother, my brother Brad, the girls, and I are crammed into the back seat of our Volkswagen Fastback, me lying across the ledge in the back window the whole ride, a human projectile just waiting for a hard brake. In this scene we're all sitting there watching the doors intently and suddenly I hear *the voice*. The booming, ethereal, disembodied voice that echoes from the tower says something I can't quite make out but I know that whatever it was, it means that all the men (and a few women) will be coming out the doors any minute. And sure enough, my dad ambles out, lunch pail a'swinging, the one that looks like a plain, skinny, black barn.

My brother asks him if he has anything left in his lunch and he pulls out a package of pink, coconut-covered mounds of cake and marshmallow. He tears open the wrapping with his huge hands and breaks off pieces of cake for each of us, popping the last bit into his mouth.

Some years later, my father moved from Simpson Lee to Welco Lumber, a mill across the river and farther north, in Marysville, and we kids saw him even less. He began working the swing shift, 3:00 to 11:00 PM, the schedule that would dominate much of the final act in his role as my dad. Other than a few treasured memories of bedtime read-alouds and the occasional serenade as he strummed his guitar, my father's presence during those years is best illustrated by the oil-splotched empty space next to our fence in which his blue Chevrolet pickup sometimes sat.

In 1970, when I was three years old, we moved from a rental home in a more rural part of Everett to a planned residential neighborhood in the suburbs. We were part of the first wave of families to move into this development, several of whom took advantage of government subsidies to help purchase their homes. The development was named Heritage North, perhaps an homage to our struggling pioneer forebears, our tract houses circling seemingly sacred mounds of dirt in cul-de-sacs like wagons protecting the last standing trees. (For some reason, years later, our neighborhood would inexplicably be renamed Heritage West, causing my friends and I to suddenly question all that we had assumed about the geography of our little world.)

The cul-de-sacs of our neighborhood sprang from the main drive like leaves from one long, slightly curving stem that snaked its way lazily through the development. The houses in each had been designed and built by the same contractor, so each cul-de-sac was a jumbled replica of the one across from it. There were three styles of houses: the one-story rambler, a rectangle with a carport on one side and a windowless wall on the other; the split-level, where families could coexist without ever actually seeing one another; and the model we had, the two-story A-frame, a house that was mostly roof from the front and mostly triangle from the sides.

The fact that our neighborhood was structured in such a predictable way created an often surreal experience for me as a child. At any given time, I would find myself in a sort of *Bizarro* world of my own, visiting a friend whose house was identical to mine only with a reversed floor plan, better-groomed pets, and nicely coordinated furniture. I'd walk through the rooms, thinking to myself, "This is what our living room would look like with orange shag," or "It's amazing how a wall of mirrored tiles makes the dining room look huge." But strangest of all was the relative peace and quiet I'd often find in these homes, a sense of calm that was seldom present in my own. I could pretend that there had been a switch at the hospital where I was born and I'd gone home with this family. Same house, different family. A father who mowed the lawn on weekends and wrestled with his kids and a mother who passed out Kool-Aid like it was pouring from the faucets. In some cases, I think my friends played the same imaginary game. They liked to come to my house so they could play hard and not worry about tearing up the yard. They tolerated the occasional sting of a sprouting thistle or the unpleasant discovery of a forgotten pile of dog manure because there was no one yelling at them to ease up on the lawn.

On the surface, my memories of childhood seem idyllic. Summers in our neighborhood were long days of darting through the woods that surrounded us, undeveloped land filled with alder and cedar perfect for nailing salvaged plywood and pallets into a crude fort. Sticks were guns, pinecones were grenades. We came home when our mother yelled for us, hands covered in pitch that would have to wear off in its own time. Our summers were more or less a predictable montage of weekend camping trips, hikes to the nearby lake and—one highlight—the annual Welco Lumber company picnic.

The gathering normally held few surprises. We kids would be free to roam the park near the lake where we could keep busy all day and out of our parents' hair, darting back and forth to and from the red plastic treasure chest of normally forbidden sugared drinks. My father appeared in cameos on these days—this, the one day of the year that I ever saw him drunk. He'd disappear into the crowd of men holding brown bottles, the swoop of a red R on the labels; we'd see him pop up between the shifting shapes of his buddies, shades of red growing deeper in his face and eyes by the hour until at last my mother would gather us kids and help him into the van as he happily channeled Johnny Cash. Strangely enough, those moments in my memory are calming, my father happy, silly, no risk of him suddenly losing his temper and angrily swinging his arm at the passengers behind him.

*　　*　　*

July of 1978. I had turned eleven years old three months earlier and this would be the last summer of my parents' marriage. Everyone at the picnic knew that my father and Kelly, a nineteen-year-old coworker, were having some kind of intimate relationship. About four days before the picnic, a friend of my mother's who worked at the mill confided that there was indeed "something going on" between my father and a woman on his shift. That night, my mother drove to the mill and confronted my father. He denied it, tried desperately to explain it away as just a rumor, but when the lies finally collapsed under their own weight, he had no choice but to admit it was true.

I remember seeing Kelly for the first time at the picnic, though I wouldn't realize her significance in my life until much later. I noticed her at the picnic because the coziness, the familiarity she seemed to share with my father was something I'd not seen before, not even with my own mother. A laugh, a playful sock to the arm, a gentle touch to his lower back. She didn't look like the kind of person my father was typically with. A woman in Levis, flannel shirt with the sleeves ripped off, no hips, long stringy black hair, she was a tomboy who looked like she had more in common with my brother than my father. I gravitated toward the two of them where they stood surrounded by men from my dad's crew and my father introduced me. I was excited to finally meet the man I knew over the CB radio as the Great Pumpkin, and when my father drew my attention to Kelly, his tone changed. It was softer, expectant, as if he were showing me a new car he'd bought, something of which he was supremely proud and would likely be using with care for some time. She said "hi" in a quiet voice, stealing a look at me and glancing around nervously, as if the two of us were doing something horribly wrong. I heard my mother call my name and her voice was completely the opposite of

Kelly's, stern and direct. I turned and hustled away, understanding that I had intruded on the adults long enough. The jungle gym was calling me now.

*   *   *

"The picnic was at Lake Goodwin that weekend," my mother explains. Understandably, the last thing she wanted was to go to the picnic that day and she didn't see the need for the family to make an appearance. "I think it's stupid," she'd told him. "I don't want to be there."

He pleaded with her, telling her he *had* to be there. "I'm on the planning committee and they're expecting me," he said, and it became clear to her that if she dug her heels in too deep, he might go on without her. So she relented, agreeing to go on the condition that my father do absolutely nothing that might humiliate her.

"The first thing he did was start drinking beer from the keg there, which was unlike him because he didn't usually hit it so hard so fast," my mother recalls. "Then Kelly showed up." The other picnickers had noticed Kelly's arrival too, and a portion of the crowd became like spectators at a rumble, nervously looking between my father, Kelly, and my mother, waiting for the shoe to drop.

At some point my mother began walking toward the lake, passing Kelly on her way down. "I want to talk to you," my mother said sharply. She walked on with Kelly a good twenty feet behind her. When they were a safe distance from the crowd, my mother turned around to face her. "You need to know that if he leaves, we don't have the income to support two houses," she said. "And then there's child support. I only have a part-time job." Kelly looked over my mother's shoulder and my father suddenly appeared, seemingly from nowhere.

"What's going on?" he asked. My mother glared at him, turned and went back toward the picnic.

As the day went on, my father continued nursing the keg. "I was standing around, trying to look like everything was great," my mother says. "The Kentucky Fried Chicken dinners had come and most everyone was sitting down at picnic tables, eating. Suddenly, I looked up and there was Kelly leaning against someone's pickup truck with a beer in her

34

hand." My father stood between my mother and Kelly, facing his new young girlfriend with a beer in one hand; the other was planted against the truck, next to her head.

"I guess I just lost it," my mother says matter-of-factly, and the rest I remember with an oddly muffled clarity. I don't recall seeing her run at him like a linebacker, her arms stretched out in front of her. Nor did I see her slamming into his upper back, pushing him right into Kelly. But I do have a distinct memory of the crash, the yells, and beer flying in all directions. Across the table from me was an older gentleman with bushy eyebrows and thinning hair slicked back over his head like a scarf and he was frozen mid-motion, his fork halfway between his plate and his gaping mouth.

"I told you not to embarrass or humiliate me!" my mother screamed at my father. Whirling around, she stomped over to our table, where my sister Karen and I were eating. "Get your brother and sisters; we're leaving *now*," she ordered.

We left the picnic with two empty seats in our van: my father's and my fifteen-year-old brother Brad's, who had been nowhere to be found (he'd be dropped off later at the house, stumbling and retching from the effects of too many stolen beers). As I quickly packed clothes into a brown paper shopping bag for a long weekend at my grandparents' house I heard a car door slam. I pressed my face against my bedroom window just in time to see my father walk sheepishly through the gate. The front door opened and my mother stepped out on to the porch.

"I don't think you have a clue what you're doing," she told him. "But I want you to get your shit out before I get back on Tuesday."

*   *   *

Like logs turning into lumber, what has once been viewed as sturdy and reliably forever often finds itself carved into something completely new and different. The massive red cedar, towering, majestic, and seemingly eternal ultimately finds itself lying flat on a hillside, limbs being methodically torn from its sides, its bark eagerly stripped away. Change can cut to the quick in a dangerously sudden motion; the spinning blade of the band saw shapes a massive trunk to fit other needs—studs for a house, a row of fence posts, the beveled frame for a cherished family portrait. I could never have fathomed the significance then, but as I returned home from my grandparents' house that day my life would be forever altered. The blue Chevy truck was gone from the cul-de-sac, never to return with any real permanence. And for an eleven-year-old boy who adored his mother but feared a father he barely knew, this change would be at once terrifying and strangely exhilarating.

CHAPTER 9

DECEPTION CAN BE A PERCEIVED or literal means of survival. People create lies to further their own agendas or simply to keep out of trouble. I'd grown accustomed to lies and deception in my family, and over time I'd grown equally used to the reassuring outcome when the truth eventually emerged. It never really took much effort, finding the real story. No one in my family has ever really been good at keeping secrets. For my sister Karen, the truth rests just behind her lips, like the air inside an overly inflated balloon. The slightest hint of suspicion is a pinprick that bursts the truth forward, the relief of confession the reward she's been wanting so badly.

My mother will often weave her inventions like a fine tapestry; the term "lie like a rug" describes it most appropriately. I inherited this talent from her. We prefer to avoid complication by covering with a white lie, a minor story to explain our forgetfulness or our lack of efforts. Rather than simply say, "I couldn't make it," or "I just wasn't feeling up to it," we feel compelled to spin a tale that will explain, without a doubt, that we had no other option but to make the choice we did. My tooth broke on an ice cube. I had to wait an hour to get it fixed. The car broke down on the way back. We pack our stories with impossible detail, choosing to embellish an untruth rather than say nothing, thinking that we are doing our listener an unselfish service by not requiring him to fill in his own details. I've made great progress in overcoming this tendency, I'm happy to say. I think both my mother and I have. We've learned over time most people don't need detailed reasons for the trivial choices we've made that may have affected them. A simple apology will suffice 'and if they need more, it's not our problem.

My father builds lies like an apartment building might be built in haste and desperation, thrown together with no real foresight or skill. The foundation is weak, crudely constructed. Each story added places greater strain on that initial foundation until the weight of that last lie is simply too much. The entire structure gives way, crashes down around him and he is exposed. The greater problem is that too often my father continues to build, unaware or refusing to acknowledge that there is nothing left on which to construct his world. His credibility is laid to waste and only the most desperately needy who still surround him continue to live within his created fantasy.

I think it's human nature to lie, to use our imagination to create a scenario that will serve as an escape hatch from a misdeed, or perhaps create the dream of a truth that we wish might have been. My son tells me that he didn't take a cookie, yet crumbs adorn his face like a beard. He wants to avoid getting punished. A student of mine claims he left his homework at home. He's hoping for another day to complete it. No real harm done by those actions or the lies, other than a small lack of trust from the recipient. It's not like someone died.

But sometimes a lie can lead to the worst of consequences. A lie can hit a nerve in the sharpest of ways, inciting an insatiable hunger for revenge and retribution, deafening the listener to any sense of reason. A lie can divide and cripple an entire population: laws can be passed, a culture can be altered, an entire community can be destroyed by a single false accusation. It happened that night in June of 1920. Two teenagers created a lie that would result in the deaths of three men. No official reason for them having told this story has ever been given. And that lie would remain dormant, festering and poisoning generations to come.

Years after the night I discovered this story, I would have the opportunity to speak with many people who from their own perspectives helped give me insight into why it had all happened. At this point, though, I could only try to formulate my own understanding. Not only did these two individuals concoct a story of rape, not once did they waver in their account. Why? What was it about Irene Tusken and Jimmie Sullivan that, even as their own stories collapsed around them, crushing others in the scattered debris, caused them to hold firm?

For me, the greatest irony of all is that in spite of literally hundreds of pages of recorded documents—court transcripts, detectives' reports, newspaper articles, interviews, Michael Fedo's meticulously researched book, *The Lynchings in Duluth*—that question has never been answered. I dove completely into the mountains of paperwork, broke down the details point by point, and reconstructed them into a narrative that came alive for me. And in this quest I was able to place myself as closely beside my great-grandfather—as close to the lynchings—as I possibly could.

TWO

CHAPTER 10

THE NUMBER OF PEOPLE coming to West Duluth from the outlying neighborhoods had been unusual that night. The number of passengers crowding onto the streetcars always rose and fell throughout the day; weekend nights could be especially busy when there was a good show playing at either the Orpheum or Lyceum theaters. But the night of June 14, 1920, had not been a typical Monday for Duluthians. As in most American towns of the time, when the circus came calling, there would be no other activity in mind. Advance men had come through town weeks earlier, pasting up posters and lithographs announcing the coming menagerie of wild animals, sideshow performers, clowns, and acrobats. The ninety-seventh tour of the John Robinson Circus's Ten Biggest Shows had been touted as the biggest show that the busy Minnesota shipping and mill town had seen in recent years. For Irene Tusken, just eighteen and fresh out of business school, the circus would have been the perfect place to steal away with her two girlfriends and, more important, to meet up with a particular boy.

Irene said that she left her house at about 8:00 PM. She and her two companions, Eudora and Dorothy, walked the three blocks or so to Grand Avenue, climbed aboard the streetcar, and rode eastward a mile to the Vernon Street stop just past the circus grounds, backtracking a block or so to the open fields west of the Missabe Ore Docks. The looming clouds that had been threatening rain all day lingered without effect. Irene marched intently with her friends toward the huge archway and commanding wooden sign that beckoned curious patrons to view the wondrous sights contained beyond the grand entrance. The litany of the barkers rose above the banter of the crowd and the lolling organ-grinder's tunes, luring wanderers to the sideshow tents to see Madame X's Snake Pit, the Human Skeleton, and Sweet Nellie Lane, the fat lady. In the menagerie, patrons could marvel at Madame de Marce's Educated

Baboons, troupes of trained seals, high-stepping ménage horses, and Virginia, the Smallest Elephant in the World.

It probably wasn't the twinkling canopy of lights that caught Irene's eyes, though; it was more likely the handsome young man standing just under the archway grinning at her. Dashing, sly, and completely full of himself, Jimmie Sullivan was the kind of boy that many a young lady wanted and most parents dreaded. With a penchant for pranks and defying adult authority, Jimmie had come to appreciate the luxuries that popularity and privilege could get a person and he made full use of those advantages whenever he could. The cigarette dangling from his lips raised the ire of morals-conscious adults and the interest of eager schoolgirls, and he'd stamp it out for no one.

The eldest of five children and the first of only two daughters, Irene had both forged a trail for her younger siblings and tested the limits of her beleaguered parents. William Tusken, a veteran Duluth mail carrier, had no doubt heard through the grapevine on his local route that his daughter and young Mr. Sullivan had been stepping out together and he'd have surely been well aware of Jimmie's reputation. Folks around the West End talked freely and the gossip was too good to ignore. A shoe merchant who was interviewed about Jimmie's character, a man referred to in an investigator's report as Mr. Blodgett, had been less than flattering in his portrayal. "Mr. Sullivan is a man of evil repute," he'd opined. A year earlier, Jimmie had broken into Mr. Blodgett's summer cottage on Lake Superior with a party of other young men and girls and ransacked the place, smashing furniture and tearing up the linens. Another man, a Mr. Pearson, corroborated the story. He'd gone to the cottage with Mr. Blodgett and witnessed the damage himself, including "empty beer and whiskey bottles all over the place." Irene wasn't spared the rumor mill. Mr. Blodgett readily repeated what was frequently whispered among the other shop owners on West and Central Avenues, that Miss Tusken "had been running around with several men and was of loose morals." Mr. Tusken may or may not have been aware of the rumblings about his daughter's indiscretions. Still, Irene was an adult with a steady job. How could a man keep control over someone who wouldn't be controlled? He and his wife had their hands full enough with four other children between the ages of four and twelve. Like many an independent woman in a suffrage-celebrating era, Irene was likely going to do what Irene wanted to do and that was that.

While both Irene and Jimmie would characterize their meeting in depositions as "accidental," the coincidence would be all too obvious as Irene had run straight to Jimmie and both Eudora and Dorothy quickly disappeared with a small group of boys standing nearby. The young couple made their way beyond the entrance, meandering down the alleyway that led the crowd past the sideshow tents on the left and the popcorn wagons and hot dog, snack, and souvenir stands on the right. They wandered on, stopping, contemplating the lure of the signage and half-heartedly agreeing that none had been interesting enough to warrant entrance. As they reached the end of the path approaching the menagerie tent, Jimmie nodded toward the big top. He asked Irene if she wanted to go in.

"No," she told him. The sharp whistle of the 9:00 curfew blasted. Ahead of the couple, circus workers led animals from the menagerie tent back to their wagons farther on back from the show, to the train waiting to take the company northward to the town of Virginia. Here and there tents sagged and poles slid from beneath lumpy canvas, hoisted upon the shoulders of brawny roustabouts to the delight of loitering onlookers. Jimmie pulled at Irene's hand and the two quickly stole from public view. A small roadway, just wide enough for a single wagon, snaked behind the remaining tents; it led from the park entrance to the railroad tracks far beyond the shadows of the big top.

The circus employees would have been busily occupied with their takedown duties; the only squads of men who may have had a moment for recreation at this time were the menagerie workers (those who worked with the animals in the show) and the cook-tent staff. A favorite activity to occupy their time: dice. A person wandering off into the trees behind a raucous big top was quite likely to stumble head-on into a fiery game of craps.

Perhaps it had been a flask of booze tucked in Jimmie's pocket, maybe the opportunity to duck into the low ravine for a momentary tryst with his girlfriend. It could have been the telltale hoots and cusses of a crap game running full blast in the distance that had drawn the young couple to another of Jimmie's tempting vices. A space of time—less than sixty minutes—becomes a puzzling mystery, a foggy narrative of conflicting stories, brazen, clumsy lies, and unanswered questions that grow more baffling with the passage of time.

Irene and Jimmie reappeared several blocks west of the darkening circus grounds, on the front steps of Merritt School just off Fortieth Avenue West. They sat together, likely recounting the events of the last hour, formulating what they might tell others later. A match lit, the smallest of fires began to smolder.

At about 10:30 PM, William Tusken was sitting in his easy chair, finishing the evening edition of the *Duluth Herald,* when he heard talking outside his front porch. While he'd later claim that he didn't recognize the male voice, it seems unlikely that he did not know to whom his daughter was speaking. Even though she'd left with her girlfriends, Mr. Tusken could hardly be so naive as to believe that Irene wouldn't have rendezvoused with her boyfriend at some point in the evening. Irene slipped inside, passing her father quickly on her way to the stairs.

"I'm going to bed," was all she said to him. His response was nothing more than an obligatory grunt. Upstairs, Mrs. Tusken was already in bed. Irene stopped by her door and poked her head inside. "Mama," she whispered. "I met Jimmie tonight and we went to the circus."

"All right, dear," her mother answered. "Go to bed, now."

*　　*　　*

The chimes of eleven o'clock signaled Mr. Tusken that it was time for him to fold up the paper and turn in for the night. Meanwhile, less than two miles east across the railway tracks, Jimmie changed his clothes for his midnight shift at the docks. He was a boat spotter; his job was to stand out on the dock watching for incoming boats. As they came in, he would direct them into the proper landing, known as a pocket. The constant dust and smoke could be irritating to the eyes and sinuses, but it wasn't hard work. And a full billfold was a gold key for a young playboy like Jimmie.

The Sullivan household was always a whirlwind of activity; like Irene,

Jimmie was the eldest of several siblings. In his case, there were five younger brothers and sisters, the youngest boy just age six. One can imagine that the middle of the night was one of the few quiet moments in the house.

Patrick Sullivan, Jimmie's father, also worked at the docks. According to his testimony, he was already working at his desk when his son arrived at midnight. He was used to seeing his son here and there during his shift, so when Jimmie stopped in to speak with his father over an hour into his shift, Mr. Sullivan likely thought nothing of it. Until Jimmie began talking, that is.

He had gone to the Robinson Circus with his girl earlier that evening, Jimmie explained (this would have been no surprise to Mr. Sullivan; so had almost every other person in Duluth). While strolling innocently on the grounds behind the tents, he continued, several "niggers" had approached the couple, blocking their path. One man had grabbed Jimmie, another stuck a gun to his head, telling him that if he moved, he'd have his head blown off. And then, if that wasn't enough, four or five more of them had carried Irene off and *ravished* her as he'd been forced to watch. He'd wanted to stop it, he concluded, but what could he do?

Mr. Sullivan was naturally incensed. A fire swelled in his gut as he picked up the telephone. He was embarrassed that his first conversation with William Tusken would concern something so heinous; still, the introduction was unavoidable, however unpleasant. When he reached Mr. Tusken, he kept the conversation brief. He told the girl's father that he understood something had happened that night at the circus grounds involving some Negroes and that someone should speak to Irene before any further actions were taken. Mr. Sullivan added that he'd appreciate a call back as soon as possible.

Back at the Tusken home, William awoke his wife Amanda with urgent instructions that she speak with their daughter immediately about that night's events. Amanda did as she was told; Irene recapitulated the tale that she and Jimmie had formulated. Amanda carried the heartbreaking news to her husband who, in turn, returned Patrick Sullivan's call.

"What do you want done about this?" Mr. Sullivan asked the girl's

45

father. "This is a case for you." The response was unintelligible; William's voice broke in an emotional quandary. He agreed that the police needed to be called in immediately.

*   *   *

Over four hours later, Duluth police chief John Murphy would telephone the yardmaster at the Duluth, Winnipeg, and Pacific Railway station-house with orders to stop the outbound train. Jimmie had told his story in full, lurid detail a second time that night. Six colored men—circus workers—had raped his girlfriend Irene, he'd told the chief. The assault had been so violent that she'd been barely able to walk the few blocks to the streetcar. Murphy called the dispatcher at the police station. "Get hold of Fiskett, Schulte, Lading, and Olson," he demanded. "Find ten or twelve others and have them meet me at the Duluth, Winnipeg, and Pacific lines in West Duluth right away." Daylight had yet to break as the officers ran clumsily down the tracks to the waiting train. The men breathlessly questioned the urgency of this raid, taking pains to keep their footing as they jogged alongside the rails. "There were six of 'em," called Murphy, his stomach burning with indignation. "Six circus niggers raped a white girl."

Twelve hours later, a half-dozen young black men languished in cells at the West Duluth police station. One of them was twenty-four year-old Elmer Jackson. The former enlisted man, a veteran of riding the rails and the frenzy of circus life, was inexperienced in dealings with the law. Elmer sat in solitude, confused, frightened, and unaware of the more ominous happenings outside the cold brick walls that surrounded him and his cellmates. A growing mob, driven by mad rage and vengeance was marching through the streets of the West End toward the jail. Its numbers multiplying, overtaking the weak and isolated, it hid all-too-well the cowardly followers disappearing securely into its mass. What would soon land at their doorstep, reaching for them through the walls of their cages, these captive targets could never have imagined, even in their worst nightmares.

CHAPTER 11

THE HIMALAYAN BLACKBERRY is a frustrating, suffocating plant that I love very conditionally. Throughout the year it invades my space and envelops the ground where the things I've intentionally planted beg to receive sunlight and water. It's a selfish monster. Its massive roots store nutrition and suck up water that is desperately needed by other plants. Vines reach out from the shadows, hanging over the paths on which I walk, and snag my shirt, my hair, the flesh on my arms. Cutting it back, even down to the dirt, is like shooing an annoying housefly from the table. Before you realize it, it's back.

One month of the year, though, the blackberry brambles pay off, providing the succulent reward for having allowed it to exist. The sweetness of blackberries transcends the sticky, dusty days of late summer and every pint of syrup, every pie, each thick blackberry milkshake masks the truth that the host is nothing more than an invasive weed, dropped into place by whatever bird or mammal ingested its fruit and, soon after, shat its seeds into the soft ground beneath the salal.

*　　*　　*

It didn't take long for my mother to move on from my father. About a week after he moved from our house into an apartment with his new girlfriend, a new man had planted himself on the couch of our living room. His concrete-encrusted jeans powdered the green plaid upholstery; his gritty boots sat propped on the edge of the coffee table, scratching the chipped varnish. He'd made our home his home, enforcing rules that had long since gone out the window and commanding full control of the television remote. In the oil-stained spot next to the fence where my father's blue Chevy pickup had once been was a rusted yellow Pinto with one broken taillight.

Lenny was not an imposing figure at first sight. Slight of build, he walked with a hunched-over, slack-necked gait, his hands in his pockets more often than not. Jaw firmly clenched, his mouth was peculiarly drawn and it was only when I accused him of mumbling an inane question to me that I found out that he had no teeth at all in his lower gums (my mother confided this to me—his response to my inability to understand him was to call me a "little bastard" and send me to my room). His dark receding hair was unkempt. Swirled and wind-caught even when the air was dead calm, it gave him a slightly mad look, not unlike Jack Nicholson pecking maniacally at his typewriter in *The Shining*. Except for the short time between a wet combing and his quick walk out the door to the bar, I became accustomed to Lenny looking like he'd just come in from a monsoon.

Like my nemesis the blackberry, the first several weeks with Lenny were sweet and rewarding. He could be generous both with his time and money when the situation suited him. Gone were the boxes of powdered milk to which we'd grown accustomed; occasional stops for burgers and fries became a semi-regular event. Invitations to car races or to play chess were opportunities to bond, I thought, and even when barbed insults and acidic sarcasm dug into me, I brushed them aside, ignoring the stinging pain and keeping my eyes on the fruits that this man displayed so unabashedly.

In the beginning, he'd been careful and calculating, as if he were sizing up the competition he'd have in this new home of his. He'd ask confusing questions, for which there were no real answers.

"What do you think?" he'd ask.

I'd answer, "About what?"

"About anything," he'd say. Then I'd be lost and he'd have no mercy. An incredulous cry of ignorance on my part and he'd wind up with a monologue about how the schools were teaching me nothing, I had my head up my ass, I'd better get my act together.

"What'd ya get done today?" he'd ask, forcing me to take a mental inventory of the day's activities and if there wasn't enough substance, enough work to satisfy the boss, I'd hear about it—for hours.

The roots he slipped silently under my own sapped the emotional strength from my limbs with guilt and shame and cut off my access to whatever support I could get from my mother. *Mama's boy, puss,* and *fatty* were his terms of endearment, brand-new and gifted especially for me. In hindsight, I can see that he entered our family as if it were a game of chess. He'd watch and wait, sizing up the weaknesses of his adversary before deciding just how hard he could push and with what mind-manipulating tool. He made it his mission to envelop my mother as his own, recognizing that her own great issues of codependency could be exploited to meet his needs. Within a month, "my father's kids"—Julie, Brad, and Beth—would defect to my father's new apartment to live with him and his girlfriend, who was just a year older than his eldest daughter. Karen would find that life was much easier if she spent four nights of the week at a friend's house. My mother and Lenny went out often, came home late, and shared a relationship of which I couldn't even begin to be a part. Healthy or not, my mother had a new life for herself and I just didn't fit in as easily as I had before.

By summer's end, the deceptive gleam that came with the promise of change had disappeared. I'd been duped, fooled into thinking that this new direction that my mother was taking us, this new man who would be taking over the role of father, would fix everything. He'll take an interest in me, I had hoped. We'll be pals and he'll guide me through life without terrifying me with a surprise temper. Instead, I was left with an overwhelming thicket of nasty thorns and I was trapped, worse off than I had been before. Now I was alone.

*   *   *

Lenny had two sons from his first marriage, Danny and Jason, who appeared at our doorstep every so often, I suppose about one weekend a month. Danny was ten years old, a year younger than I was, and he was the boy that I knew Lenny had hoped I'd be. He was athletic, cocky, and full of energy. Jason was about two years younger than Danny and a bit more like me. He was pudgy and whined and was a convenient target when Danny and I felt the need to take a potshot at someone else. It was on their first visit to our house that the ugly, complicated world of grown-up relationships, marriages, divorces, and new-found lovers became sordidly fused in my naive brain.

The brothers and I zipped in and out of the trails—our bikes were motorcycles, we were soldiers, freedom fighters escaping the clutches of the Nazi war machine. A quick dash and a hard right off the trail and we were in the safety of a cathedral-like cedar grove. Dismounting, we propped our bikes against a fallen log and sat down. Jason set off to pick up pine cones, collecting them in the apron of his T-shirt as ammunition for a later assault. Still gasping for breath, out of the blue, Danny said, "You know they're doin' it, right?" He looked at me slyly, smirking. "My dad and your mom."

"No, they're not," I said. They weren't married, after all, so how could they be? "They just sleep together, that's all."

Both boys laughed, belly laughs at my ignorance and reddening face. "Yes they are," Danny insisted. "You're stupid if you think they're not."

The knot in my gut raged and I contemplated slugging him, knocking him from his bike. I thought I might just bolt from the scene, race home to my mother so that she could set this absurd story straight.

"You're stupid," I retorted. "My mother wouldn't do that." The last thing I wanted, like any eleven-year-old boy, was to think that my mother would have sex with anyone—least of all the thing living in our house right then.

"Fine, don't believe me," Danny said, laughing. "You'll see." And as quickly as the topic had been raised, it was dropped. We were off, set to do battle against the marauding invaders once again.

The next morning, the three of us sat in the living room together, the previous day's conversation more or less forgotten, our bowls of Cheerios heaping and *Scooby-Doo* flickering from the television. Suddenly I heard my name being called from down the hall, from my mother's bedroom. It was Lenny's voice.

"Coming!" I answered, shuffling on down the hallway to her room, leaving my cereal on the TV tray to soak.

From behind the door, he told me to come in. I opened it just a few inches and peered inside. Lenny and my mother lay in bed, the covers pulled tightly to my mother's neck and just above Lenny's waist. The drapes were drawn closed and the dull glow of daylight crept over the curtain rod, just enough to illuminate the sickly whiteness of his bare skin.

50

"So I heard you have a problem," he said, nearly in a whisper. The swirling blue smoke belching from his and her companion ashtrays threatened to envelop them both completely.

"No."

"You don't?"

"No," I repeated.

"Hmm . . . I see." His voice was calculated, taunting, and I imagined there must be a slight smirk at the edges of his mouth. I looked at my mother and I could tell that her head was turned slightly, her eyes directed somewhere past me. "You weren't whining about your mom and me sleeping together?"

"No," I lied, heart racing and cheeks flushed. My throat began to tighten and my eyes welled.

"Well, I'm here now and you're just going to have to deal with it," he said, a little louder. By now I could see that his gaze was direct and unmoving. Battle lines were clearly being drawn and he had just thrown down the gauntlet. He took a drag from his cigarette and the orange glow from the tip lit his face in a frightening mask. The room fell back into the shadows and I watched the cherry drop to the ashtray. "What are you crying for?"

"I'm not," I mumbled.

"Oh really?"

"Yes. I yawned a minute ago, that's all."

"You're a mother-fucking liar," he growled, leaning forward in the bed. "Get your mama's boy ass out of here."

I closed the door behind me and stood for a moment in the hallway, waiting for my mother to appear and console me, apologize for the jerk of a man she had been feeding and sheltering and allowing to crowd her children from the house and from her arms. It didn't happen. There would be no remorse communicated, nor a sense that any was forthcoming. He was in deep, his roots firmly planted and consuming as much around him as he could and it was at that precise moment that the new landscape of my life opened up in front of me.

CHAPTER 12

I WALKED INTO MY MOTHER'S CONDO and dropped a stack of papers on her dining room table, knowing that in minutes the leaves of all that she had believed about her family tree would be shaken loose from the branches, to fall around her in scattered chaos. She sat down and reached for the printouts; I pulled them back toward me.

"Before we go through these," I began warily, "do you know if your grandfather was ever in prison?"

She paused for a moment, then shrugged her shoulders. "Well, not that I know of," she replied matter-of-factly. "Although I wouldn't be surprised. He was a drinker and I'm sure he crashed around a lot in his younger years. Why? What did you find?"

"Well, I found some things that might be upsetting to you," I said, "that say . . . he might have gone to prison for a short time, for some rioting and . . . stuff."

"Rioting? Over what?"

I spread out the material and allowed her to soak in the headlines, handing her the *Ripsaw News* article first. Her eyes narrowed, folds of skin raised sharply along her forehead. Her lips parted very slightly, and she shifted her body to one side and leaned forward, propping her elbow on the table and resting her chin between her thumb and forefinger. When she reached her grandfather's name—and I could see the exact moment it had touched her—she drew in a sharp breath, and I stretched my arm across the table and gently laid it on her forearm.

"Oh, Pa," she sighed, taking off her glasses and rubbing her eyes wearily. "What happened?"

We moved through the story together, combed through the copies of archived news articles slowly, methodically. I'd read them already, backward and forward; my mother ran her finger along the text, her focus intense and steely.

"I was frightened and filled with dread," she would tell me later, much later, when we finally took a few moments to talk about that day. "There were so many questions coming up that I knew would—and could—never be answered."

Before I'd arrived that day, my mother had brought out the familiar small metal briefcase from her closet. After a dozen moves—from house to house, apartments, a trailer—this was what remained of any mementos of my childhood, my family's past. A jumble of snapshots and school report cards kept loosely in one container, never catalogued into photo albums since it had been easier to keep track of a single larger item rather than five small ones. Clearing the space in front of me, I dumped the contents of the case onto the glass tabletop.

It was the Polaroids that grabbed my attention first, with their thick white borders and glossy washed-out faces. Most were of Lenny standing by a car, Lenny with me, Lenny with Karen, our adolescent faces pimply and strained, filled with discomfort and self-consciousness. I grimaced and said something about the mop of a hairdo I'd had then; my mother laughed and said that we all had had more hair then. I turned up a single photo of my father, standing at the sink with his father in the background. In it, he's wearing a white shirt and looks very young. My mother sucked in her breath, looked away, and I pretended not to notice.

I dug through the pile, pulling up the old pictures that I'd seen many times before but whose subjects now stirred a renewed interest. Many faces remained unknown, familiar ones called out loudly as I set them aside. A postcard from Bennett, Wisconsin, one from Solon Springs. A few studio portraits labeled West End, Duluth. Suddenly a particular snapshot caught my eye. A posed shot, my Grandpa Ray seated in the cab of an old Ford pickup. He must have been about twelve or thirteen and I remembered having looked at the photo years ago, when I was twelve, imagining myself in the same spot. The truck, decorated for what may have been a parade, patriotic flagging draped like bunting along its sides, was adorned with a sign that was suddenly more meaningful than it had been before: *City Transfer.*

The newspaper articles we'd just read had referred to the truck driven by Louis Dondino, a truck he drove when he did transfer work for the city of Duluth, collecting mail from the rail stations and making general deliveries. *This could be the very truck that he drove to the jail,* I thought, and now the idea of placing myself in the cab made my ears ring. Pulling the photo closer, I squinted at the face of the young boy in the passenger seat. He was smiling at the cameraman—probably his own father, Louis—and he looked proud to have been propped up high, a few feet up from the street in this shiny new Ford. A moment of joy, a prelude to the unimaginable that was just months away.

I looked again at my mother and I understood the pain and confusion on her face. I knew it was going to take some time for her to come to a realization that she'd been duped, that a person in whom she'd placed her utmost trust and admiration could have done something so inhuman. In some way—not on the same level, but in a parallel world—I had been where she sat now.

I thought of my own father. I pictured myself sitting in his truck, looking admiringly at him from the passenger seat, my head cocked and straining to decipher the gravely voiced ramblings over the CB radio in his blue Chevy, its dashboard covered with soft carpeting, glued on to match its exterior. My father takes the microphone into his hand, presses his thumb against the button, and barks, "This is Chevy Blue with the Little Quacker at his side looking for the Great Pumpkin, ya got yer ears on?" That had been a moment of joy, too, alone in the cab, me and my dad.

Early visions of my father remain a contrast of personalities, each flickering in my memory like movements against a strobe. Hearty laughter, his singing along with the gentle strum of the guitar, and the soft lull of his voice reading from a novel before bed clash jarringly with the flash of clenched yellow teeth, sharp brow, and red-ringed eyes, belt slipping from his waist and swinging at his side as he stomps toward me.

As the father of a young son, I beam at the memory of my own child's firsts: that initial plane ride after his adoption, his tiny body curled up in my arms as we crossed over the Arctic Circle from Moscow to his new home in the United States; that cool November afternoon when he toddled to the edge of the water, gazing at the expanse of the ocean for the first time in his young life; the first time he had the words to tell me at last

54

what was on his mind. It's especially rewarding to be able to lay claim to having provided or at least encouraged these things to happen for him.

My father owns the privilege of taking me on my first camping trip, buying my first fishing pole, and cleaning my first trout. He also holds the title of having issued my first black eye, bloodied my nose for the first time and having broken my front tooth with his own hands—all before I had reached the age of ten. The lesson I learned from these times was that a leather belt was actually preferable to fists because one could more or less count on the whippings staying below the waist. No belt meant that his hands would land on whatever parts of my body happened to get in the way and when Dad was mad, there was no telling how wildly or how hard he'd swing.

*   *   *

Walking around the garden at my home in Kingston, I feel like I'm a million years away from anything that can hurt me. It's the unexpected reminder of nature's hidden assailants that alerts me to pay attention to my periphery. As in life, I've come to be wary of the tendril-like nettles that often drape unexpectedly over the well-traveled paths in my garden, delicate tall stems and feathery flowers waiting for the light brush of bare skin. The sting of the nettle is both a surprise and a lingering annoyance that serves as a reminder to choose my path carefully and watch where I might be digging. Too often, as I crawl on my hands and knees to pull at the carpet of weeds in the underbrush of my garden, I am stunned by the shock of a nettle sting. The acidic hairs of the stem and underside of the leaves do exactly what the plant intends—provide a reason for others to stay away.

*   *   *

I stare at the photo of my grandfather in his newsboy hat, his innocent grin, peering out the window of his pa's truck and I wonder how much longer that innocence will last for him. Soon, he would be stung in a way that will resonate throughout his entire life, causing him to create a path that would lead him far from his own father. The pain of memory would send both men hundreds of miles from their roots, hoping that new ground might give them solace from the welts that stubbornly remained on their souls, painful and burning. They could leave the source of the hurt behind, but the seeds would remain hidden just below the surface, and sure enough, these nettles would find their way back among the new plants. Mine would lay dormant for years, coincidentally appearing to wound me around the same time in my life as they had my grandfather.

*　　*　　*

A horror story envelops many families as they frantically hack workable paths through the thickets of divorce. Through a child's eyes, this experience can be suspiciously delightful, though no less confusing and uncomfortable as the dark elements of the true narrative come into view, the deceptive façade of pleasantries and promise fading into the background.

The Invasion of the Daddy Snatchers. The character of Suddenly Absent Dad metamorphoses, somehow achieving a position on a pedestal, where he blossoms in his new role as an every-other-weekend parent. Frozen pizza, sugary cereals, and free reign of the television set turned my father into a dream dad. And it didn't hurt that I could complain freely about Mom's new boyfriend and he'd be visibly indignant at how this man was mistreating me (both of us conveniently forgetting the various injuries I'd sustained from *him*; or perhaps my father was bothered that another man had the gall to try and take his place). At any rate, my father's and my outings to the wrecking yards and hardware stores took on a new style and I didn't even flinch at his slights of hand, the secret pocketings of a hood ornament or crescent wrench when no one else was looking. "These things are write-offs for them," he'd say matter-of-factly. "It's not like I'm not spending enough money here as it is."

*　　*　　*

Up until the winter of 1979, there wasn't a lot that my dad could have done that would have surprised me or made me judge his character any differently than I already had. I knew the back of his hand as well as the front, and even at the age of eleven, I regarded any potentially impressive story he might tell me through a gauze of pessimism. My father embellished and exaggerated. I didn't care. It's not like anyone got hurt by it.

Until the day I heard about the Big One, the one offense that would threaten to pull the rug from under him once and for all. It had snowed pretty hard a few days before; *that* I remember with vivid clarity. I can see myself stomping out of the apartment building (to which we'd moved with Lenny a few months earlier) and even though it was past dark, there was the eerie look of twilight as happens when the rising moon jumps off the newly powdered ground, the deceptive look of daytime as the brilliant expanse around tricks one's mind by drawing white linen curtains over the deep blue shadows of an early nightfall. It's a calming image that, even now, soothes my nerves. And it was the peace that I so desperately needed on that day.

Mine was an eleven-year-old mind trying to make sense out of what, up until thirty minutes earlier, had been a twelve-year-old secret. I reached into my canvas *Seattle Times* bag and grabbed a tightly rolled newspaper, my numb fingers automatically releasing it to land in the right doorway. My motions were mechanical, my emotions randomly firing while I searched for the ones that seemed like they were supposed to fit a moment like this.

I strained to picture my father as I had thought he was, not the man my mother, my sister, and the two women who had been waiting in the apartment were painting for me. The reality was, as much as I thought I'd figured him out, I didn't know my father at all. The people who fished my carelessly flung newspapers from their shrubs were more familiar to me than my own father. I hurled a paper up to a balcony and struggled to think of something nice, some source of warmth as my freezing feet carved ruts in the slush, my second-rate sneakers soaked through the fake leather, and for a second I wondered if my mother would be mad that I had worn my school shoes on my route.

Stupid, really. I realized then that every image I brought to mind in which my father was smiling, he was always looking away—at the road ahead, at his fly cast in the rippling pond, gazing at the snapping flames of the campfire and squinting against the smoke. "Smoke follows beauty, y'know," he'd say, his eyes gazing past me, into the trees.

The apartment had been dark, all the drapes drawn, and a single lamp next to the sofa had barely given off enough light for me to see that the phone had been left off the hook. My sister was crouched on a chair in the corner as the two women talked to me, women I'd never seen before and would likely never lay eyes on again. "I'm from the sexual assault center," one of them had told me, as if that explained it all.

Tell me what will happen now? my mind screamed. Karen wouldn't look at me but I stared at her dagger-fierce, refusing to turn away. I'd wanted her to crack, to see that I knew she was lying, that she was only saying this about our dad because she wanted attention. She'd been running away from home at the drop of a hat since our dad had moved out and it had stopped generating much of a reaction in our house, and since he wasn't living with us, what better way to get attention than to say that he had done horrible things to her? And besides, if it was true, how could I not know and why in the hell hadn't she said something before?

How dare you tell these lies now that we are living alone in this apartment with glitter on the ceiling and a long hallway outside the door that always smells like someone else's cooking and I know it will never smell like Mom's cooking because macaroni and cheese doesn't smell like anything. I hate the moss-colored shag carpet and I hate sharing a bedroom with my sister and I hate the smell of someone else's Crock-Pot stew.

All I could think then was that I needed to leave, deliver the papers before it got too dark and the customers started calling. I thought I might change my shoes, put on my raggedy boots, but then I said to myself, *What the hell I just want to get out of here away from these women.*

I really can't pin down when I finally put the pieces together, when I figured out that Karen wasn't lying and that the liar was my father. I know it wasn't on that day, but perhaps it had been within the month, maybe a little longer. It might have been when I began to think carefully about the bedtime read-alouds and how none of my sisters ever seemed to know a thing about the stories he'd read to us, and they'd even gotten angry when I'd talked one too many times about *Bambi* or *Where the Red Fern Grows.* I would never have guessed that bedtime meant something else to them.

My dad, always the storyteller.

It's hard to embrace the nettles that spring up in one's life, especially when they appear in gardens that should be places of solace and trust. For years, I'd wanted so badly to give my father the benefit of the doubt, to allow the excuse of generational poisoning—the intrusion of those toxic, painful seedlings that have sent runners through my family for decades—and forgive those who have managed to choke those of us within their reach. But some things skate precariously close to the line of unforgivable, so close that words like *rights* and *justice* become blurry and hard to place into the context of real life.

Perhaps the crowd that night in Duluth classified the rape of a young woman as unforgivable; maybe the anger magnified to such a degree that reason and logic were trampled underfoot. Lies swirled like a dust storm then, as they do today, and if time isn't allowed for the particles to settle and the view to become clear, people die. "It could be your daughter or your wife," someone had shouted as the rumors rolled over the streets of Duluth. In my case, on that numb, dark-blue evening, it was my sister. And I didn't know what to do.

CHAPTER 13

LIKE BURRS TO WOOLEN SOCKS, tagalongs clung to the Ford truck as my great-grandfather Louis wound his way through the streets of West Duluth. "Come on, show what kind of men you are!" one young man had shouted from inside the bed of the truck. "The niggers raped that girl, and she might be dead!" Others worked even harder to get to the core of the bystanders' fears, egging them on to action. "What if the girl had been your wife or daughter?" They had been furious—one of *theirs* had been violated by one of *them*. Eventually the crowd spilled over the sides of the pickup bed and onto the streets and by 6:00 PM a sizeable mob was accompanying the truck, which by now was just six blocks from the jail. One group of young men dashed into Siegel Hardware across from the police station to gather several yards of rope. The clerk on shift had handed over the rope free of charge. "You're doing a good thing," he'd told the men. An officer on his way to his shift at the jail, a man named Victor Isaacson, walked past the crowd. "Mr. Isaacson, bring the niggers out," someone had yelled from the truck. "We want them!"

Inside the jail, six black circus workers would listen to the growing rancor outside with increasing uneasiness. Despite reassurances from the officers on duty that they would be safe, the fear and anxiety in the faces of their jailers must have been all too obvious. For Elmer Jackson, what had begun as a confusing case of mistaken identity was swelling into a matter of life and death.

On this day, several crucial pieces of information would be conveniently cast aside, ignored, or perhaps just misunderstood. Two of them may well have prevented the police from stopping the circus train at all that night. Jimmie and Irene had essentially waited hours to come forward with their tale. Their conversations on the night of the supposed assault had been filled with standard fare, uninteresting, until Jimmie casually reported the rape to his father well after midnight. Even so, the police would accept the accusations without question.

Then there was the fact that Jimmie Sullivan had been far from a model citizen, certainly not a boy who would have been any prosecutor's first pick as a prime witness. But the most upsetting detail is one about which there is no speculation, no question of inconsistency with what had been described by the couple. Irene Tusken's own family doctor would examine her in a most thorough and certainly uncomfortable manner. The physician's reflections of the examination are shockingly unremarkable in his obvious conclusions that no apparent signs of trauma existed. Dr. David Graham made this very clear when contacted by one skeptical detective. "I don't think she was raped," Graham told him. When interviewed for the evening edition of the *Duluth Herald* that night, he was quoted as saying, "I believe she is suffering more from nervous exhaustion than anything else."

These details neither reached nor mattered to the growing mob waiting outside the station doors. Their ferociousness was fueled by another misunderstanding that was spreading widely. A group passing by the

Tusken home had asked Irene's mother, who was standing on the porch, how her daughter was doing. She replied, "She's in bed," which was unfortunately received as "She's dead." It wouldn't be long until the rioting crowd numbered nearly ten thousand.

Inside the jail, the small crew of policemen struggled to keep composed as the situation outside spun out of control. An earlier break-in attempt through the garage doors at the back of the station had been thwarted, but the officers' options were severely limited.

"I don't want to see the blood of one white person spilled for six blacks," ordered police commissioner Bill Murnian (coincidentally, the uncle of Louis Dondino's late wife Nellie). They were forbidden to use firearms, so the officers desperately tried other means to maintain control of the quickly collapsing situation, using a hose to douse the crowd in front of the entrance and scattering rioters like leaves from a walkway.

A fire truck managed to snake its way through the crowd, parking at the front of the building. Additional officers ran to it, grasping at the fire hose. A surge of angry men pushed forward, wrestling with the police and firemen for it. Louis Dondino lunged at an officer, warning him, "Don't you dare touch that hose! Those men are doing good work!" Within minutes, the mob overpowered the lawmen and commandeered the hose, turning the weapon upon its hosts, washing away the few uniformed men left at the front of the station.

Hurled rocks, water blasts, physical batterings ensued until the officers on duty could withstand no more. The final barrier was broken as a hole appeared directly through the brick-and-mortar wall. A crowd of victorious vigilantes spilled in, followed by gallons of spraying water.

In the cells, the prisoners would wait for what must have been a growing obviousness of their doom. Crouched in the shadows trembling, some stood mute in disbelief. Lonny Williams, curled up, childlike, in a ball beneath his cot, retched and vomited as the realization of his hunters' discovery hit him. Their jailers' reassurances hours before meant nothing to the prisoners now. Upstairs, twenty-year-old Isaac McGhie, terrified and pleading, was dragged from his cell in the boys' division and beaten unmercifully. Blood flowed from his mouth and broken nose; he spat out a tooth as he begged for his life. "Oh God, oh

God, oh God. I am only twenty years old. I have never done anything wrong, I swear I didn't. Oh God, my God, help me." He collapsed in their grips, urinating in his pants before being flung into Elias Clayton's cell.

The vigilantes wandered through the building, collecting men like sheep, corralling them into a single pen before their final judgment. Elmer Jackson waited quietly beside the cot in his cell; reports say he appeared merely curious at the unrelenting banging and wrenching at his cell door. Plucked from where he stood, he was thrown among five other prisoners into the single cell, where an even more surreal event was taking place.

The white men overseeing their beaten, bloodied prisoners pressed them against the cell wall, like a lineup for a firing squad. "We're going to find out which nigger's guilty," one man yelled. "We want to be fair!" And thus the "trial" began.

"Now, which one of you did it? Out with it!"

"Come on, talk damn you!"

"Who was the man with the gun?"

"Never mind the questions, let's just kill these niggers!" someone suddenly shouted. "The militia will be here before we can hang 'em!"

A resurgence of movement, white men grabbing black, and the first of three men was pulled from the cell and dragged to the street below, where the mob waited. Isaac McGhie, the one prisoner not arrested for the alleged rape (he'd been identified and held as a "material witness"), continued pleading his innocence to no avail. "So help me God," he sobbed, "I did nothing and know nothing."

He and Elmer Jackson were hurled from the station onto Superior Street and passed roughly from man to man until they stood naked from the waist up, their shirts hanging torn from their bodies, war paint of the blood from their faces streaking down their dark torsos. As they were dragged up Second Avenue East toward First Street, wild men and women lurched forward, clawing, spitting, punching, and kicking at the men in a gauntlet of unbridled fury. On the corner, a boy of nineteen held a precarious balance on the lamppost; he'd shinnied up the pole earlier in search of a perfect vantage point for the calamitous goings-on down the street. Now they appeared to be heading his way, a development the boy neither expected nor appreciated, and he began to scramble down, eager to escape from the deadly events that were coming too close.

"Toss this rope over the top, kid," came a gruff, authoritative voice from below. The boy hesitated, torn between what his churning guts were telling him and the angry screams from the mob below. He looked down at the bloody, terrified face that suddenly appeared at the base of the pole. The boy held the rope in his trembling fingers. It was inescapable. He was to be the final instrument of execution in this horrible saga. The mob howled, goading him on.

Isaac McGhie begged for his life, praying for divine intervention. Father William Powers, a Catholic priest, tried desperately to shout some sense of humanity into the crowd.

"Men, you don't know this man is guilty," he shouted as the rope suddenly dropped from the lamppost under which several men restrained Isaac. "Let the law take its course," Father Powers implored. "In the name of God and the church I represent, I ask you to stop!"

"To hell with the law!" was the crowd's response.

"Lynch him!"

"Remember the girl!"

The noose was slipped quickly and methodically over Isaac's head and in seconds he sailed upward. He stayed aloft only momentarily and then dropped to the ground, the rope suddenly slack. His relief would be cruelly brief as the crowd quickly cinched the rope again, raising him just a few feet from the pavement. His dying gasps fueled the crowd's lust for more blood.

Elmer Jackson moved stoically through the crowd as his executioners led him to his gallows. As he was positioned next to the hanging body of Isaac McGhie, he gazed calmly and resignedly at the second noose dangling above his head, then let his eyes scan coolly the white faces glaring back at him. Reaching into his pocket, he drew out a pair of dice, letting them sail defiantly to the ground. "I won't need these anymore in this world," he said firmly.

A young man in the crowd retrieved them and offered them back to Elmer. "Well, you might want to roll them in the next," he sneered.

It's hard to imagine what must have gone through Elmer's mind in the final moments of life, what thoughts brought him to his stoic acceptance of his fate. Witnesses reported an eerie sense of calm in his demeanor in those last few moments. Perhaps he believed that for whatever reason, the Lord had deemed it time for him to leave his earthly existence. A sharp pull, his feet left the ground, and he swung grotesquely next to his fellow victim, his body convulsing in its dying moments, his ears deaf to the cheering and whistling that accompanied his death.

A third young man was dragged forward, Elias Clayton, pleading futilely with the crowd, which chanted mockingly, "Lynch the third one! Lynch the third one!" A punch to the face, a quickly cinched noose, and Elias shot into the air higher than either of the first two men. As he twisted and struggled, gasping for air, a thug clinging to the pole swung a kick at him, catching him squarely in the face. The rope was fastened to a spike, suspending Elias above his fellow murdered roustabouts.

"Throw a little light on the subject!" came a cry from the crowd, and someone swung a car around to face the lamppost, training its searchlight on the morbid scene, illuminating the mob like hunters showing off their kill.

Elias's body would at last be cut down, not as an act of mercy, but to facilitate a better shot for Superior photographer Ralph Greenfield. Dozens of men gathered around the dead, smiling with pride and exhilaration as if posing at a postgame rally.

"Send them pictures to Alabama," one person called. "Tell 'em to keep their niggers."

Someone might have done just that. Soon after the lynchings the photo would be printed on postcards and offered for sale in several retail outlets in and around Duluth. The cards would sell out within days.

CHAPTER 14

I CALLED MY MOTHER as soon as I finished reading Michael Fedo's chapter on the lynchings; the pivotal event in his book that illuminated each of the players in that horrible scene at the lamppost. She'd gotten through it the night before and had been waiting for me to catch up before we talked. The scene of the lynchings had loomed for us as we read the accounts of the riot, waiting to see when and where Louis would appear. We were relieved—just a little—when he wasn't placed at the street corner where the hangings took place. Still, the two of us were lost and unsure of what we should do, or even feel, next.

My mother kept saying over and over, "There isn't anyone to talk to about this." No siblings, no cousins with whom she could discuss the story and the fact that so much of her life had been cloaked within one horrible secret was like being trapped in a house of mirrors. Everything she thought had been real was now distorted, a false image created by a warped sense of reality.

"I wish I knew if my mother had known about it," she said, her voice breaking into a whimper. "I just can't believe that they'd have been able to keep something like this hidden. The people I lived with all those years, with angry outbursts a regularity and not much being sacred. And never a word about this revealed. I'm thinking, 'Did I ever really know them?'"

I said maybe they knew it would be too painful for her to hear, that they believed they were protecting her by keeping a secret. "They didn't want you to know about the evils of the world, I'd guess. Murder and rapes were things they didn't want to talk about. They wanted to keep you innocent." There was a long pause and I asked if she was still there.

"I don't think I ever told you about this," she said suddenly. Her speech was slower, contemplative, and I knew from the tone that this was going to be new to me. "I was about ten, and the old man (her father) was friends with this guy named Tom Casey," she said. "Tom was an alcoholic and so was his wife Lena. They had two sons, Rudy and Nicky." She went on to tell me about Rudy, that he'd been a year younger than she and that the two had played together often, sometimes spending the night at one another's house. "I remember that when I was there, Tom liked to stay up late watching *Friday Night Fights* and *The Liberace Show*."

As the story unfolded, she began to describe one night in particular, when she and the two boys had been left alone while Rudy's parents had gone out drinking. "I wasn't worried," she said. "The tavern was just up the street." Late into the evening, after the television had been shut down, the kids settled in for the night. She lay asleep on the couch and Rudy had been slumbering next to her, on the floor. Mr. and Mrs. Casey stumbled into the living room after having closed down the tavern, loudly whispering and shuffling their way into the back bedroom. A few minutes later Tom came back into the room. A cough and a low chuckle roused her from the cloud of near-sleep and she'd opened one eye slightly. "The porch light was shining through the front window," she told me. "And there was just enough light that I could see him coming toward me. He was wearing just an undershirt and boxer shorts."

"He said, 'I'm gonna tickle you,' and all of a sudden I could feel his hands on me." He'd grabbed her sides at first, then let his hands roam freely along her body. She'd lain frozen in terror, her own arms glued to her sides as his rough hands groped, rubbed, and squeezed. "I could feel something against my leg moving back and forth and I knew even then what it was. The whole time, Rudy kept laughing because his dad was still tickling him with his other hand."

And as quickly as it all had begun it was over. He'd pulled back and walked nonchalantly back to the bedroom. She'd remained rigid with terror and helplessness. "I thought for a minute about jumping out the window and running down the alley for home, but I didn't know how I could explain why I had left." She couldn't tell anyone—who would believe her? And even if her story had been accepted, she imagined that she'd surely be in trouble. "I thought they'd say I was to blame because I laid there and let it happen," she said. Staring at the ceiling, she waited until the dim break of morning before she slipped from the couch, gathered her things, and nudged Rudy awake. "I gotta go home now," she whispered. "My mom said I gotta come home now."

And like the bundle of clothes she clutched protectively to her body as she'd slipped quietly down the alleyway in her pajamas and into the still-sleepy morning silence of her own house, my mother had held this secret to tightly to herself. Night after night, nightmares threw her from her slumber, but her whimpers into her pillow went unnoticed until one night my grandmother happened by my mother's room as she lay crying. She opened the door and slipped inside.

"What's wrong, honey?" she asked, sitting on the edge of the bed. She rested her hand on her daughter's leg gently, patting her arm with the other.

"Nothing," my mother lied.

"Oh now, don't tell me nothin'," my grandmother said. "A girl don't lie in bed cryin' over nothin'."

Coaxing, reassuring, sincere promises poured from her mother and finally my mother told everything, describing in detail what she'd seen, what she'd felt, what had been done to her. Stunned, my grandmother left her daughter's side and returned to the kitchen, where my grandfather sat nursing a beer.

"I don't believe that," he grumbled, after my grandmother had re-counted the story. "Tom's my friend and he wouldn't do anything like that."

"How come she knows all this stuff if it didn't happen?" My grand-mother was adamant in her attempts to convince her husband that their daughter had been molested. For all her pleadings and demands, he just wouldn't hear it.

"It's in her head."

My grandmother returned to her daughter's side, patting her shoul-der. "It's all right, honey."

"Daddy doesn't believe me!" my mother cried, embarrassed, betrayed.

"I don't care," her mother seethed. "I believe you and you need to stay clear away from that Tom. Rudy can come and stay overnight here and he can play here, but don't you go over there any more to play." Her voice trembled, cold and hard in a way that my mother hadn't heard from her before. "And I don't trust that Lena, either. Her bein' a woman and all and she's just as big a drinker, just like them men!"

My mother took a deep breath, signaling the end of her story, and I voiced amazement at this revelation. "I hadn't thought of it in a long time," she said. "I know I stopped having nightmares about it right away." I asked her why she didn't feel like it had been weighing on her mind all these years. "I think it made all the difference, what your grandma said then," she answered. "That she believed me, no matter what."

I wanted to know then how my grandfather would have reacted to the news about my own father, and what he'd done to his daughters. I knew that neither of my grandparents had been told the truth. When my father had gone to jail, his parents had simply been told that it involved a teenaged girl they didn't know. I wanted to know if my mother thought her father would have believed the story this time.

"Oh hell yes," she says. "That was why I didn't tell them. Your sister was your grandpa's treasure." My mother muses over the uncanny parallels between her father's bond with her daughter and the one she remembers with her own grandfather. "No, if he found out, he would have driven straight to your dad's place and put a bullet right through him, there's no doubt in my mind. I knew it then and I know it now. And if the news of your sister didn't kill your grandma, that definitely would have."

CHAPTER 15

"I NEVER LIKED BRINGING FRIENDS TO MY HOUSE," my mother tells me. "My dad's behavior was so embarrassing and I always thought my house was a dump." Summers brought a welcome reprieve, since my grandmother could spread a blanket on the grass, present a heaping basket of sandwiches and cookies, and her friends could have a picnic lunch, never having to set foot in the house. "And there were a couple girlfriends of mine who thought my dad was a riot when he had a few under his belt. I'd be mortified and they'd just laugh. 'He's *so* funny,' they'd tell me."

I can relate to this, since I never liked bringing my friends to my home once Lenny was in the picture. It wasn't the piles of engine blocks, rotting lumber, and boxes of building supplies scattered throughout the back-yard, nor was it the occasional sounds of creaking bedsprings and banging headboard that emanated from his and my mother's room above mine. It was the unrelenting way in which Lenny liked to put me on the spot, making a show of his control over me to the amusement of my friends.

"You probably know how to cut and stack wood," he'd say to one. "Maybe you can teach Warren how to do it right."

"Don't you think Warren walks just like his mother?" he'd laugh to another. "Warren, walk to the kitchen and back. Watch him."

"So," out of the blue he'd ask his favorite rhetorical question, "what do you think?" The visitor would be as perplexed as any normal person would, looking around the room for some kind of reference he was referring to. Lenny would laugh and I'd whisk my friend from the room, giggling like a nervous schoolgirl about what a weirdo my stepfather was. Some would be courteously dismissive, others seemed genuinely amused by it all, thinking him harmless, that he'd been simply tossing sarcasm that was more entertaining than creepy. In time, I would stop bringing any but the most understanding of peers, usually kids whose own parents were further into the shadows than mine, those who seemed never to be home at any hour of the day or, when they were, tended to slip ghostlike from sofa to kitchen to bedroom without so much as a single word to their child's friend.

*   *   *

As my father's trial drew near, I withdrew from my friends even more. I'd maintained a couple of close relationships, though even they remained in the dark about the drama slowly unfolding behind me. I'd tried to shut out the particulars of the trial as much as possible, push away any reference that my mother or my counselor would make to it. I had known that there would be a hearing and that there was a chance that my father might go to jail. I also knew that there was a distinct possibility that he would not, and that there was a list of factors that could place the results on one side or the other.

My mother did the best she could under the circumstances to look out for me at this time, I know this now and I knew it then. She'd ask me how I was handling things, I'd say fine. She scheduled me for counseling sessions to work things through and rather than spend the time processing feelings about my father, I complained about Lenny. As the trial kicked into gear, my sister Karen began to make daily trips to the counselor, the attorneys, and the sexual assault advocates, and it was all my mother could do to manage a home, an inconsistent husband, and a daughter who was dealing with more than any human should ever have to bear.

The one time I let it overwhelm me, I sat in my room in the dark, pulling the elastic from my socks and imagining any number of wishes I might have been granted that would make things normal for me. I began to fold into myself, and the still silence and the blackness around me gave a sense of calm that I'd so desperately been craving. I wanted it to last and last and then the thump of footsteps grew loud and I knew that my moment of meditation had ended. Lenny swung open the door and hovered in the opening, quiet for just a second, suspiciously eyeing me. He asked what I was doing and I told him, "Nothing." Bullshit, he'd said and when he pressed me to tell him why I hadn't yet cleaned up after the dogs I told him that I was thinking about my dad and wondering what was going to happen to him.

"I think you're using it as an excuse," he said. "This counseling thing is all about keeping you busy so you won't think about it, so you need to quit thinking about it." He flipped the light on and pushed the door open the rest of the way. "Now go out and pick up the dog shit."

*   *   *

If he'd admitted it, if he'd taken responsibility for what he'd done, my father could have gone on with his life, gotten some treatment and kept a five-hundred-yard distance between himself and any of his daughters. This would have been the best solution all around, but it would have required the truth—the whole truth—and that was something my father had seldom been able to pull off at any time of his life. Months later I would sit in the witness chair, looking out at a smattering of faces looking back at me and dissecting my every word, and as much as I had rehearsed the teary dialogue, imagined the swelling music and glossy imagery, I soon became painfully aware that this was nothing like the movies. The attorneys didn't ask me if I loved my father. They didn't ask if I liked him. They didn't even ask if I thought he'd raped my sister.

"How old are you?"

"Thirteen," I said.

"Please speak into the microphone."

"THIRTEEN." The sound of my own voice suddenly booming through the courtroom startled me. I said my name and pointed out my father in front of me as I was asked to do.

Did I remember the weekend that he babysat us after he'd moved out? Yes. Yes, I remembered that he had been there.

Is that all? I asked myself. *Ask me more.*

Ask me if I remember being told to stay outside and play even though it was pouring rain and all I wanted to do was play in my room with my Hot Wheels.

Ask me if I remember trying to come inside to go to the bathroom but the doors were locked and even though I rang the doorbell over and over no one would answer.

Ask me if I knew they were home and couldn't understand why they would ignore me.

Ask me how I felt standing outside my own bedroom window, my pants wet with piss, crying because the window was locked and when was that stupid window ever locked anyway?

Yes, he had been there that weekend, I repeated, when the defense attorney asked me the same question, her tone doubtful and accusing. I glanced nervously at my father and there were the all-too-familiar red eyes and the disappointed shaking of his head.

His voice is smooth as silk. I can hear it even now and I feel like he's in the room with me, watching as I write this. I see the old, shredded copy of *Bambi* and hear the voice that I must have listened to a hundred times for the clarity it still has in my memory. "It is 'He,'" the story warns. "Bambi's mother cautions him of the very dangers of the nature of man." I'm eight years old, and my father is seated at the foot of my bed, his right leg crossed over his left, softly reading to me at my bedtime, my favorite book of all. *"Ever since we came into the world He's given us no peace, but has killed us whenever we showed our heads."* And his voice is filled with compassion and pacifism and empathy, while in the back of his mind he's waiting to leave my room, climb the stairs to the girls' bedroom, and commit the unthinkable. And I look back at this scene with adult eyes and his paternal warmth is tainted with filth.

I feel the anger from a crime unforgivable and I know how it aches to want retribution or even death for another person but then I pull away, force myself to see the human behind the monster. I look up and imagine what will never be. His clear blue eyes are smiling back at me, gently and with pure honesty. His arms embrace his terrible acts with true remorse and accountability and his love is so genuine and healthy that his apology rings like the bells of a cathedral for the entire city to hear at last, at long last.

CHAPTER 16

ADOLESCENT ANGST IS aptly named. Every tiny incident, each malady that sets one apart from his peers (in reality or simply perception) is cause for plunging into the depths of darkness. I see it in my eldest son now and then, and I can only hope that he's nowhere near the place in which I often found myself at his age. I used to lie awake at night, staring out the window and imagining all the places I could hide, how to get away from my home and the crippling exhaustion that came from knowing that I was trapped, that there was no way out of this situation except through time. I'd count the years left until I graduated high school, then break those down into months, then weeks, and finally days. The math got easier the more often I did it and before long I had the first part of the problem memorized. Two and a half years. That's thirty months. That's only one hundred and thirty weeks. Nine hundred and ten days. Nine hundred and ten days. Tomorrow will be one less.

I'd wondered what would happen if I caused Lenny's death. Since his luck seemed completely unwilling to give out, no matter how many times he got behind the wheel with a .3 blood alcohol content, I imagined scenarios in which I might help things along. I imagined crushing pills into his whiskey, I fantasized about taking the tiny .22 pistol from his nightstand and "accidentally" squeezing the trigger in his face the next time he flipped on my light at 3:00 AM. "I thought it was a burglar," I'd say. "He scared me." More than anything, I wanted to be free. Then I'd let it go, fully aware of the impracticality of it all. I'd go to jail, my mother would be devastated, and I really would have amounted to nothing. Lenny would have been proven right and would have won even in death. Strangely, logic always overrode ethics when I drew these conclusions; it would be many years before I would grasp the concept that killing Lenny would be not just logistically impractical, but morally wrong.

If I had shot him, I'd not have been the first in my family to kill a man under the cloak of self-preservation. Another item I'd discover much later in life was that my grandmother's father—my mother's *other* grandfather—had once shot a man dead in self-defense. On October 29, 1901, my great-grandfather Malcolm Foy had been serving a writ of attachment to a farmer by the name of Crenshaw in the small town of Decatur, Mississippi. As a local attorney, it was one of his duties to deliver notices of foreclosure. The farmer had been expecting this and he and his eighteen-year-old daughter Savena greeted my great-grandfather with a hail of gunfire. Malcolm had taken cover and returned fire, killing the farmer and injuring Savena.

My grandmother would never share the story of her father's gunfight with us; in all likelihood, she never knew. I'd have been oblivious as well had I not been poking around newspaper archives, searching for the prominent Malcolm Foy (besides having been Newton County prosecutor, Foy had served in the Mississippi state legislature from 1908 to 1912). If she did know the story of Crenshaw's killing, she'd have kept quiet on principle alone. My grandmother absolutely, without question, hated guns.

Despite my grandmother's disapproval, my grandfather kept guns in the house throughout their marriage. One night, when my brother Brad and sister Beth were visiting, Brad had taken a .22 rifle from its display rack on the wall; not knowing it was loaded (who'd have thought?), he pulled the trigger, firing a charge into the kitchen wall above my grandmother's head. Fortunately my grandfather had been asleep (on his "good ear") and was none the wiser. My grandmother carefully returned the gun to its rack and went back to stirring the stew, patting her chest and fanning her face all the while.

*   *   *

When my mother was a child, her father owned a double-barreled shotgun, which he kept loaded next to the refrigerator in the all-white kitchen of their home. This apparently had not been an unusual thing in those times.

"Kids were told early on to keep their hands off guns, and we did," my mother says. "I don't recall ever hearing much about kids playing with guns." Nonetheless, it bothered my grandmother Margaret no end and she frequently implored my grandfather to at least take the shells out of the gun.

One day, tired of begging, she took it upon herself to unload the weapon. Carefully removing the shells, she secretly placed them in the kitchen drawer, ready to withstand the consequences of defying her husband's wishes once he discovered what she'd done.

A couple of days later, my great-grandfather Louis came to the house for a visit. Both he and my grandfather quickly settled into the kitchen, beers in hand and cans of snuff at the ready. My grandmother and my mother instinctively moved to another part of the house, having learned by now that when the two men drank together, the area should be deemed a danger zone and was best left alone. Time went on and the number of empty bottles grew; the volume and tempers in the kitchen began to escalate. "Oh good lord," my grandmother murmured, "here we go again."

She made her way back to the kitchen with young Nellie Rose in tow. They entered the room just in time to see Louis angrily snatch the shotgun from next to the refrigerator and whirl back around to his son Ray, thrusting it hard against his chest. Although she had done it just two days earlier, my grandmother must have spun through her memory a million times in that split second, trying to remember whether she actually had emptied the chambers.

74

As Louis pulled back both hammers, my grandmother screamed at what she would later describe to my mother as "the loudest, most horrible sounds of my life." Ray stood frozen and "white as a sheet," my mother says. Louis threw the gun to the floor and ran from the house as his son stood trembling in place.

"Is Pa mad at Daddy?" my mother had asked.

"No," answered her mother. "Everything's just fine, dear."

*   *   *

Like I've done every now and then as I contemplate the possibility of various choices we might make in the span of a lifetime, the possibilities of changing one's path, my mother would often wonder what her life would have been like had one little detail of this story been different.

"I used to think that things would have been better if the gun had gone off," she says before quickly qualifying her statement. "But I know things would have been worse—much worse. It would have probably destroyed your grandma and . . . I'm sure it would have all just been awful." And in spite of its magnitude, nothing was ever said of the incident again. "My grandpa came back to the house a few hours later and nobody said anything, things just went back to the way they'd been the day before," explains my mother. "It was like the whole thing had never happened."

CHAPTER 17

THE DAY AFTER THE LYNCHINGS and beyond, the town of Duluth seemed like it was suffering from one big hangover. The headlines in the *Duluth Herald* screamed chaos and the realization that the lynched men may have been innocent began to filter its way into the minds and conversations of those who were willing to talk about it. Heads held low, words hushed, it was obvious that the anarchy and pride that the mob had displayed in full view that night was nowhere to be seen in the light of day. There was shame growing, deservedly so, like a creeping mold overtaking the putrid remnants of murderous rage.

In spite of this realization, the rediscovery of a collective conscience, the fearful reflex of intolerance swelled in and around Duluth. Employers fired whole crews of blacks and the chief of police in Superior vowed to "run all idle Negroes out of Superior, and they're going to stay out." The continuing hysteria resulted in what would become a significant exodus of blacks from the region and a lingering cloud of racial mistrust that would last for decades.

It soon became apparent that responsibility would need to be assessed and someone was going to have to be held accountable for the deaths of the three men. In spite of thousands of witnesses, though, it was becoming agonizingly clear that not one person was going to step forward and identify the men who had placed and pulled the rope. Perhaps those who had directly carried out the death sentences were conveniently well-connected in the community. Perhaps offering a fellow Duluthian up for first-degree murder was unthinkable. At any rate, the city prosecutors knew that something must be done. Someone had to be held accountable for the chaos that night.

On August 8, nearly two months after the riots, nine men would be indicted on charges ranging from inciting the riot to first-degree murder. One of those nine would be my great-grandfather, Louis Dondino. Initially slapped with a first-degree murder charge, the grand jury would throw out decreasingly serious charges (from first-degree murder to riot) before eventually settling upon a single charge of inciting a riot.

The trial for Louis lasted barely a month. A conviction and sentence of five years at the state penitentiary at Stillwater followed immediately. In the end, only two others besides him would be convicted of any charge related to the lynchings—none of them murder, and none of them with a sentence of greater than five years.

For my grandfather, thirteen year-old Ray, this would mean the end of a great many things. School, for one; not that he'd gone with any consistency in the past, but there would be no one to force the issue now. For the foreseeable future, he'd remain in Bennett on his grandparents' farm where the emphasis would be on work rather than books. My grandfather would speak fondly of his grandparents in his later years and it was clear that his extended family had been there to take care of him as well, so there had certainly been no lack of supervision of this growing young man. His uncles Elza and George had neighboring farms and if they couldn't be the surrogate fathers that Ray needed, they would at least keep him busy in the fields. His grandmother Sarah kept a watchful eye on him, this much was certain. In her advancing years, though, she'd become less tolerant of his rambunctious energy, though her agility hadn't suffered. Sarah, at nearly eighty, was as quick and nimble as ever.

The time he lived with his father had always been sporadic and unfocused for my grandfather, though since his father had gotten work with the city prior to the lynchings, things had been on the upswing for them both. Ray's grandparents probably wouldn't have talked with their grandson too much about why his father was in jail, but he must have known. Everyone had known. Even across the bridge from Duluth to Wisconsin, in the tiny town of Bennett, people would have been talking about it. It had been in the papers nearly every day and with a name like Dondino, the family wouldn't have been able to pretend it was not their relation.

I have to believe that the whisperings of friends and strangers would have hurt my grandfather most. One minute they'd have cursed the timing of the trials, angrily questioning why white men were being tried before the surviving blacks. Letters to the editor of the *Duluth Herald* seethed with anger over the fact that the "colored men" were still in jail awaiting trial on charges of rape (the charges still stood) while the prosecutor seemed more interested in going after white men. The next moment, though, he'd have seen a shake of the head, a chastising for the animalistic actions of the crowd across the lake. My grandfather, barely a teenager, wouldn't have known what to think about it all. The only sure thing was that he'd likely be an adult before he'd ever see his father free again. I think about this and I see him again pictured in that truck, the old Ford with the tiny rectangular window behind his head, and the side slats along the bed. Now it looks to me as if he's abandoned and gazing wistfully out the window. He's alone, helpless and understandably furious at the man who has left him to fend for himself in a world where even the adults can't tell him how to feel.

Peppered throughout my great-grandfather's prison visitation log is my grandfather's name. Ray had come to visit less than a dozen times, usually with his Uncle Elza. He'd have been about fourteen years old, my grandfather. And in reading those files for the first time, I found myself feeling a sudden and unexpected connection with my grandfather, an emotional bond that I never had the fortune of realizing while he was alive.

I know what it's like to have to scratch your name into a prison log-book, submit to an uncomfortably intimate pat-down search by a complete stranger, and listen to the hard clang of a heavy iron door on the way through to visit your father. I think it would be a hard thing for any child to have to experience, but I wonder if it's not hardest on the adolescent. A young boy approaching manhood is desperately searching for a father figure to emulate, to stand as a model for what he himself will become in the not-too-distant future. For me, prison was an embarrassment, a scene of absolute humiliation as my father was reduced to nothing more than a child, punished and forced to ask permission for the most basic of things, all the while pretending that the only thing that had changed in his life was his address.

My mother would drive me up to the Washington State Reformatory to see my father about every other month, maybe more. I can't remember the frequency today. She always accompanied me into the visiting area, which I now appreciate as a true testament to her firm control over her own vengeful desires. Sitting placidly and politely in a noisy, echoing room across from the man who'd raped her daughter and two step-daughters for ten years must have been akin to a starving cat being restrained from a fat mouse lumbering at her feet. She wanted so badly to pounce, to tear him to pieces, but logic and parental responsibilities kept her at bay.

Visits with my father were an exercise in me chatting nonchalantly about my own life while he spun tales that showed him as the Steve McQueen of the medium security set. He'd point to various men in the room to create an exciting scene in prison life that involved them. He liked to try to paint himself as a respected man among the harder set, never mind what I knew even then about the life of a statutory rapist in prison (what his eventual conviction was for, given the fact that Karen was the only one who accused him at trial, that she was his adopted daughter, not a blood relation, that the trial focused on one particular weekend when she was a teenager—and his lie regarding that weekend would be exposed, clinching the conviction). I vacillated between missing him desperately and wishing he'd be transferred to a place where I'd never have to go. The security check, the guards, the prevalence of tattoos—there was nothing remotely normal about the visits with my father. Each one was a reminder that there was not one adult in my life who could help me get out of the madness of my home and the only thing he and I had in common at that point in time was that we were both trapped, each of us probably spending the better parts of our days dreaming of eventual freedom.

On an early visit to my father, just after he'd been moved from a penitentiary to the reformatory, he had shown me a crudely scratched tattoo on his arm, which read "Hawk." He'd smiled sheepishly at me, saying "It's 'cause I got a fast right hook." My mother had laughed, taking a drag on her cigarette and squeezing my arm. She leaned in close to me. "Don't repeat that to anyone," she warned.

"Why not?" I asked, but she ignored me, instead glaring pityingly at my father. *You think his friends won't know what Hawk really means?* she seemed to say as he rolled his eyes at her in response.

With the exception of one friend, whose family circumstances were eerily similar to mine, my visits to my father would be kept secret from my peers; it wasn't really the sort of thing I'd wanted to make the center of conversation. Mentioning where he lived would involve an explanation of his crime and that wasn't something I was willing to do. Sometimes I wonder if my grandfather and I would have ever been able to talk about this strange commonality between us. If he'd been able to tell me about his father, would he have patted my shoulder and told me that in time people would stop talking about it and I could just forget that my father had ever been in a place like that?

But even as I draw the parallels between my grandfather's dilemma and my own, I recognize that I had the luxury of anonymity. My father's trial would not be splashed across the front pages of the local paper and my name would not become synonymous with a scandal that would be decried in news outlets across the country. Suddenly, the fact that there are today multiple spellings of the family surname makes complete and total sense to me. Like the aftermath of an explosion, fragments of family history lie scattered throughout the Great Lakes area, connected only by my tedious research and careful reconstruction.

About ten years ago I came across an old letter that my father had written and sent to me from prison. It had been kept in its envelope and when I picked it up from a jumbled collection of papers, my initial thought was that it had been one of those assignments in which you are asked to write a letter to yourself—the handwriting was identical to my own. The loop of the R, the similar combination of block and script; it was uncanny. When I realized what it was, the identity of the true author, I buried it beneath the stack of papers again. I wasn't ready to face it but couldn't bring myself to destroy it, either; I imagined that one day I might be ready to open it, to read it from a stronger perspective.

It's taken some years but when I write my name today, I no longer wince at its appearance on the page. The mere appearance of the name Read had for so long carried the weight of pain, of sickness and unfulfilled promises. I once had been tempted to have the spelling legally changed, to escape the stigma that I'd attached to those four letters, but today I feel that I've done enough in my own right to claim it as mine, to gift it to my own son and not feel like it must be connected eternally to one unhealthy owner, the one who had passed it on to me. I hope, on some level, that there are Dondinos out there, maybe living along the edges of Lake Superior, who feel the same. I hope they write their names with pride, with large loopy signatures in bold, dark ink that they can see from across the room.

CHAPTER 18

JUST NORTH OF EVERETT, WASHINGTON, lies an extension of suburban sprawl, a town with tract homes that have spread unrestrained over what once had been hillsides of Douglas fir and western cedar. As children, my friends and I had always referred to Marysville as the sticks, Everett being the big city to all towns north (while the rest of us went south to Seattle for fun and games). Up until as recently as the 1990s there had been at least a half dozen lumber, paper, and pulp mills dotting the banks of the Snohomish River (Everett's eastern border) on its way to Port Gardner Bay (its western line). The pungent odor of an active lumber mill always gave us grist for an accusing look within the cramped space of the passing car. The towering smokestack of the huge Weyerhaeuser plant was an institution of sorts, naively nicknamed "the cloud-maker" by the young son of a friend of mine.

In addition to the lumber mills, Everett had at one time been host to another manufacturing boom in copper, lead, and arsenic, a natural by-product of the smelting process, which was used for pesticides. The Asarco smelter plant pumped and dumped the poison into the atmosphere and surrounding soils without a moment's hesitation, unaware of the legacy it was leaving for future generations. The plant was closed in 1912, and it would be another eighty years before the community would become fully aware of the mess it had inherited. In the end, an entire neighborhood would be displaced as the extent of its contamination became clear.

In some areas, white soil, riddled with arsenic, descended up to eight feet, just off the front porches of family homes. What was once a neighborhood filled with the sounds of laughing children and barking dogs became a wasteland of empty concrete foundations and hardy weeds. To rehabilitate this neighborhood, and others, would require the complete removal of contaminated yards and gardens within a four-hundred-acre section of the city. Drastic but necessary if the goal was to truly expunge the poison.

City officials, the EPA, and the directors of Asarco each tried to pass the ball, hoping someone else would take ownership of the situation. No one wanted to accept any responsibility for the current state of affairs; nobody was willing to step forward and say, "This is my burden and I will accept it." Eventually, a compromise was brokered and the neighborhood at last saw its cleanup completed; a collection of new homes now graces the area once enclosed by chain-link fences adorned with warning signs (though the outlying acreage remains polluted).

When this story came to light twenty years ago, I was living a few miles south of the former smelter site. I vaguely remember the attention given in the local papers to it, with a picture of a man wearing a dust mask as he mowed his lawn. I'd ridden my bike through there; my mother had said "Thank God we don't have to deal with that." She was happy that it was someone else's problem, not ours. Of course, what I know now is that we had our own subterranean toxins that we weren't dealing with. We'd been moving our way through life all along wearing dust masks, pushing ourselves from one day to the next, ignoring the clouds of poison that were being pumped out from ingrained dysfunction and steadfast denial. An opportunity to clean up, to grasp responsibility for a contamination laid down in the past was presented to me and I had a choice to make. Do I bury it, or do I take shovel in hand and get to work?

In my readings about the lynchings I came across references to a committee of Duluth citizens and the work they were doing to create and install a memorial to the three men who were lynched. The group believed that, regardless of the motives and reasons for the lynchings and subsequent secrecy, it was the responsibility of the current community to help clean up the poisons of the past, to embrace what their ancestors had done and make it right. A fund-raising effort had been in place for some time, an artist chosen for what looked to be a huge undertaking. In the end, an entire city lot diagonally across from the street-lamp that was used as the lynching tree would be dedicated to Elias Clayton, Elmer Jackson, and Isaac McGhie. A monument would be built in their honor, proclaiming the community's remorse for the murders and a commitment to promoting tolerance and open communication for all of its citizens.

I considered contacting the committee, though I had no idea what I might say. "I'm the great-grandson of one of the men who went to prison. I'm sorry it happened." The words seemed empty, desperate, and contrived. I thought I might just send a small donation to the memorial, sign it "From the family of Louis Dondino," and leave it at that.

The initial e-mail I sent to the committee was brief and matter-of-fact. I simply identified myself and my connection to the lynchings and expressed my mother's and my shock at having discovered our family's role. I shared my willingness to support, in any way, the efforts toward completing the monument. While I had no idea what I could possibly do, I hoped that the committee would provide me some guidance. I imagined that in a relatively rooted community like Duluth, there must be other people still in the area whose relatives were involved in the lynchings. I never imagined I might be the only one to come forward. Still, I knew that my information would be of some interest to the group, though I had no way of knowing how it would be received.

As I processed the undeniable responsibility to insert myself into the memorial, I struggled to find a rationale for doing so. Defense of the family name? I realized one thing for certain: my great-grandfather's legacy was out of balance, both in my family's minds and in the minds of those who knew of the lynchings. Our realities sat on opposite ends of the scale. In Duluth, the name Louis Dondino brought images of racism, instigation, and mad hysteria. In our family, the same name had always conjured feelings of love, gentleness, and affection. Our Louis stood on a pedestal; theirs was a footnote to a tragic story.

I also wondered many times, would the committee want to have anything to do with me? Bringing a person on board whose great-grandfather was seen to have had a major role in the lynchings could be a powder keg in an already volatile situation. They might be hoping to sanitize the legacy of the lynchings as much as possible—moving away from the toxicity of 1920 completely, forging ahead in a strictly positive way. Still, while I hadn't yet put it together in my mind, I knew that if there was a way for me to contribute a positive, healthy component to the memorial, I had the means and responsibility to do so.

Within two days, Catherine Ostos, co-chair of the committee, replied. Her response was one of incredulity, excitement, and thanks. "No one could find any record of what had happened to Louis Dondino," she told me later. "We thought it was a lost cause. We're just so overjoyed that you've contacted us." She promised to be in touch in the coming months, and I told her I looked forward to it. And that was the last I'd hear from Catherine for some time.

*   *   *

Many times over the years, I had asked my mother if she'd grown up with messages of racism. She and my father had been very vocal about racial tolerance and I didn't recall anything else coming from my grandparents' home. Still, I'd known that my grandmother was born and raised in Mississippi and from what I'd seen in movies and read in books, slavery had been all over the South, therefore everyone from the South must have been prejudiced against blacks. On the contrary, my mother said. Her mother had had no patience for racist words and had especially spoken fondly of a "negra" (she'd said it in the most affectionate of voices) who had lived in the family home after my grandmother's mother had died. Mammy, as she referred to her, was the family's cook and caretaker, a woman who had stepped in as a mother figure for my grandmother, teaching her to cook, sew, and read Bible stories.

And then there had been Black Bill. The story of his relationship with Louis helped define her grandfather's character for my mother, elevating him in her eyes to the role of peacemaker, a man of the people, certainly far removed from the image of misguided vigilante.

The story my mother shares of Black Bill, for me, conjured up the vision of a solitary dark figure shuffling up the sidewalks of Edmonds. He worked for the railroad and lived by the tracks near the water in a small shack-the Great Northern Railway provided for him. And being the only black man in Edmonds, even in 1953, Bill would have needed to take whatever perks life would give him. White people approaching him on the street typically would continue talking, taking no notice of the man

84

ambling toward them. Bill would cast his eyes down and he'd step from the sidewalk into the gutter, where he'd stand respectfully until they passed.

He'd been in his late forties when my mother knew him, a man of stocky build with broad shoulders and hands that dwarfed those of his white neighbors. His skin was very dark, so much so that one couldn't help but notice him coming from clear at the other end of the block. My mother remembers Black Bill with vague but fond memories, the gentleman who affectionately called her "Nellie Rose, ma'am" and her mother simply "ma'am." No one knew where he'd come from; as far as the people of Edmonds were concerned, it was as if the man had no past. "But then," as my mother explains regretfully, "who would be interested enough to have asked him any questions about himself back in the fifties?"

He had likely been from somewhere in the South, my mother believes, judging by the accent he'd held in common with her mother. "He spoke very respectfully, to a fault." My mother struggles to describe a man she hardly knew, but whose existence she now holds onto desperately. "You know, as though he were afraid he'd say something that would offend. He 'knew his place,' as the whites then would say approvingly."

Bill was a familiar sight in the Dondino household, his black denim jeans and pinstriped black and white railroad shirt a vivid image in my mother's mind. "His only friends in town, the only people who would socialize with him and treat him with any kind of kinship, were my dad and grandfather," she says, shaking her head at the obvious irony of the situation.

"I remember my dad gave him a black cat as a gift; he brought it over one Saturday to Bill's shack." She laughs, not sure how much of the story was embellished by her father and his friend over the years. "When my dad went to hand the cat over, it took one look at Bill and jumped away, running up the wall and out the window, never to be seen again. Bill shrugged and said, 'Well, I don't guess he done seen a black man before!'"

Now and again, Bill would be invited to supper at the Dondino house, and on more than one occasion he brought with him a coffee can filled with pennies, which he would proudly present to my mother. "Here ya go, Nellie Rose, ma'am," he'd say, handing her the canister. "You can buy yourself some candy." When the plates were cleared, he'd never fail to shower my grandmother with generous praise. "Your cookin' always brings me back to home, ma'am," he'd say.

More often than not, conversation between the three men would be accompanied by copious amounts of Rainier Beer. Bill shared his friends' thirst for and dependence on alcohol, a strand that connected the three in the present more obviously than the skeletons of the past. Bill had been welcome in the Dondino home, but the same was not always true for the neighborhood taverns. Only at certain times, under specific circumstances, would Bill dare impose his presence on the patrons. To the unknowing eye, there would appear to be neither rhyme nor reason to his understanding when the invitation was there—if he had been with either of the Dondino men, he would certainly have been allowed in by proxy. Whatever the signal was, when Bill opened the door he'd know within seconds whether he could stay. If not, if the message wasn't a welcoming one, he'd nod politely, close the door, and make his way back to his home.

My mother shares a story her father told her several times over the years, enjoying a moment of narrative glory for my grandfather whenever the subject of Black Bill comes up. The three men had been drinking at Edmonds Tavern, lining up bottles along the bar as the night wore on. There were several other men in the tavern as well, a few playing pool, most just listening to music, smoking cigarettes, and drinking beer. Maybe the laughter had gotten a little too loud for a few of them, maybe they didn't like a black man enjoying himself too openly in their company, but the mood of the group began to get testy.

"What's so funny?" someone had called over to the three men. My grandpa Ray ignored them; he was deaf in one ear, and it might have been unintentional. Louis looked over at them and shook his head, letting them know politely that it didn't concern them.

"Hey Louie," another man piped up. "Why don't you move on over here, leave the spook in the corner." Bill turned his body away from the men and faced the bar, to let his friends leave if they chose.

Louis tipped the neck of the bottle down from his lips and swallowed.

"Why don't you go straight to hell?" he suggested. "I don't need you telling me who to drink with."

"Fine by me," the man answered back. "If you want to drink with a nigger, that's your business."

Ray turned and faced the man. "Stick it up your ass," he snapped. "This son of a bitch puts out more in a day's work than you do in a week." The two men stood, locked in a momentary standoff until Louis spoke up.

"Just leave him alone," he said. "He ain't hurtin' no one by bein' in here."

The man finally stepped back and waved off the group. "Aww, I'm just foolin' with ya, Louie," he said. "Come on, I'll buy him a beer. Hell, I'll buy you all a beer."

*   *   *

As we thought now of this story, my mother and I were plagued with burning questions. When her grandfather sat in that bar with Bill, defending him against his friends, did he think of those three men hanging by their necks; did he feel sorry? In his stoic silence about the lynchings thirty years past, in his defense of a friend who was the only grown man in town who needed permission to pay for a drink, was Bill standing in for the men Louis had helped hang three decades earlier? Then and today, we know that there is no way of really knowing what was going through his mind, his heart. But the memories of his friendship with Black Bill are reassuring to us, if nothing else.

More telling than this simple story is the fact that Louis's crime and prison sentence were never mentioned in a family where tact and self-control were foreign concepts. In a home where drunken scenes included her father's oratories on the sexual escapades of the nuns and priests who had ruled his youth, absurd accusations of infidelity between his father and his wife, Margaret, attempted shootings and flying dishes, it was uncanny that no mention of prison or lynchings would ever find their way into the open. In the most heated, unhinged of moments, the truth stayed locked tight, but I can't help but wonder if it was straining just behind my grandfather's taut lips.

"I have to believe that the shame was so deep, so unthinkable, that the very subject was a line that didn't get crossed, no matter what," my mother muses. And while learning about the lynching hasn't changed the past for her, it has begun to allow her a greater insight into the complicated men who helped shape her young life. A man she once referred to as "an asshole of a father" has become more humanized today. "I feel sorry for him now," she says. "It doesn't take away the pain of my childhood, but I know that he was much more of a tragic figure than I'd realized." And an old man who seemed to do no wrong, who had always appeared to be so unappreciated by his son now stands with so many unanswered questions. To come to reacquaint herself with a grandfather she never really knew, and understand a father she could never fully love, has been an unexpected journey in and of itself.

CHAPTER 19

MY GREAT-GRANDFATHER'S TRIAL CONCLUDED and he was convicted for the crime of inciting a riot. At his sentencing hearing on February 4, 1921, he was given the opportunity to speak to the court, to give any concluding thoughts before his sentence was handed down. It was a chance to own up, to take responsibility for his actions eight months earlier.

"I am awfully sorry, Your Honor," his statement reads in the final words of the transcript, "that I got into this trouble. I never was in trouble before." To the nonanalytical, the wishful thinker, he has apologized and made amends. But he really hasn't. He is remorseful over consequence, not motive, like my son who laments that he's lost television privileges for the week rather than the pain he's caused his brother by breaking his radio. The apology rings empty and insincere.

*   *   *

On a flu-addled, feverish night in 1994 I got the phone call I'd been hoping for since I was a teenager. This call had the potential to be a turning point in my relationship with my father, a starting point to air old wounds and allow a painful, necessary healing. I'd been drifting in and out of sleep all day and into the evening, sweating out a 104-degree fever I'd been blazing since that morning. The telephone jarred me out of my daze and I swung my arm around in the dark, trying to find the receiver. Blind fumbling, a bit of cursing, and I had it to my ear.

"Guess who this is?" It was my father's deep baritone; I was mildly irritated. I hadn't heard from him in probably six months. He had the habit of calling me from out of the blue, just to see how I was, to awkwardly engage me in conversation that I'd politely, if not sincerely, reciprocate. These calls would usually skate on topics of the weather, how school was going for me, whether or not I had a girlfriend yet. Then he'd spin tales of the unlikely things that were happening in his world, what wonderfully impossible feats filled his everyday life, and then the conversation would predictably degenerate into audacious questions about my mother and my sister Karen (at which I'd stammer, "They're fine," and quickly change the subject) and his persistent requests for me to visit. About midway through, though, this particular conversation took an unexpected turn.

"Well, son, I've been doing a lot of hard thinking lately," he sighed. His voice was halting, his words carefully chosen.

"You have?" I asked. "About what?"

"My life," he continued, slowly. "I'm not getting any younger and I figure it's time I face up to the things I've done." I said nothing, waiting for him to get to what I desperately hoped he would. "I did a lot of bad things, to you kids and the girls." His voice shook as he spoke. "It was wrong and I know that I've caused them a lot of pain with it."

My heart nearly exploded in my chest with excitement and relief. At last. At long last, the man who had been king of denials, lies, and excuses was taking responsibility and owning up. I sat up in bed and let out a long breath, rubbing my watering eyes.

"You don't know how long I've been waiting to hear you say those words," I whispered. "Thank you so much." And I was sincere—I really was proud of him for taking this step. At that moment, I actually felt that we'd turned a significant corner in our relationship and there was a real possibility of something good coming. My mind flooded with the hope of a new era, one in which the positive, beautiful aspects of my father that I'd diligently mined over the years from the hardscrabble of negativity could flourish.

"You know what would help," I pressed, "what would make all the difference in the world?"

"What's that?" He asked.

"Karen has made so many gains in her life toward getting healthy," I told him. "But she needs to know that you are sorry, that you don't hold her responsible in any way." There was silence at his end, but I kept on. "If you would simply write her a letter, just a short note telling her how sorry you are and reassuring her that it was all your fault, that would mean more to her than years of therapy."

"I already did that," he said defensively. He was frantically backpedaling, a toddler running from a quickly rising tide. "I told her that a long time ago." This was a lie; I knew he hadn't. If he had, I'd have known. Still, I took the bait.

"Really?" I asked. "Huh . . . I hadn't heard."

"There's a lot you need to know," he went on. "I was under a lot of medication for my back during those years and I was also drinking way too much. I didn't always know what I was doing. And the girls were so wild, too, and for Beth and Julie it was really only one time, anyway. . . ." His voice trailed off, becoming the familiar squawking static that I'd learned to tune out years before. My stomach sank as the sound in my ears receded to a dull monotone.

"Okay Dad," I said. "Listen, I'm not feeling well, I gotta go. Good talking to you." And I hung up.

CHAPTER 20

I HADN'T BEEN AFRAID OF BLACK GIRLS until seventh grade. It wasn't like I'd known many, to be honest. In my old neighborhood of Heritage West/North, the only persons of color I'd ever seen were the Japanese woman who'd lived behind us (with her Caucasian husband and their children) and Mrs. Varnell, the Vietnamese woman down the street, brought to the United States when her husband, Steve, came home from the war. With the exception of a couple of my mother's social-service clients, I couldn't say that I'd ever known a black girl.

"Black girls run fast." My sister Karen would say this after every track meet. "I hate running with black girls, they're always too fast. It's not fair." So the one thing I knew about black girls was that I could never outrun one.

When I met Dawnita that first week of junior high, I hadn't been afraid of her. Like me, she played violin and just like me, she'd been saddled with the second violin parts. No matter; we made jokes about the first violinists behind their backs and shot dirty looks to the teacher behind hers. But on the day that I made a joke at her expense, a slight comment about her hair that I hadn't intended to be an insult (I thought she'd gotten a new hairdo, she'd actually not had time to style it before school), all the wrath that could be pent up in an adolescent girl was unleashed on me. Slowly, in regular doses throughout the year, Dawnita would terrorize and pound me every chance she got.

It had started as simple retaliation for my comment that morning. Cornering me in the instrument room, she stared me down, a cobra waiting to strike. "You can't just up and say that to me," she commanded. Her massive arms gestured dramatically from her sleeveless shirt, her head bobbing back and forth to punctuate the seriousness of her words. For a final exclamation point, she slapped me so hard across the face that my ears rang.

The satisfaction of having put me in my place was a high this girl could and would not let go of. Day after day for the next eight months I was to be her mouse, a timid, chubby white-boy mouse from the south-end cul-de-sacs, and she the stalking cat, friendly and purring one moment, hissing and lashing out the next.

It was our not-so-secret game, our routine at orchestra practice at least twice a week. I'd show up to class, lead weight in my stomach, and evaluate how the rest of the hour would go based on the first thirty seconds of interaction with her. If any of the other girls in the class were up for some cheap entertainment, they might toss in a comment to try and get Dawnita to perform.

I fantasized about fighting back, slamming my fist into her face and watching the bright red blood pour from her dark, flat nose. I imagined grabbing her stiff hair and shoving her body into the bricks. I wanted to do it so badly, but as much as I now hated black girls, at that moment in my life I was terrified of them. Dawnita had friends, other black girls who yelled and laughed and pushed each other and threw wads of paper at other kids walking past them in the halls. She also had an older brother and he was big and walked with a bounce and had huge hair with a red pick sticking out. While I knew I could get a good lick in with Dawnita and I might be able to avoid the other girls (since I certainly couldn't out-run them) I wasn't so sure about her brother. There was no way I could take him.

So I stuck it out until the last day of school and when autumn and the new school year rolled back around, fresh white blood entered the mix. A half-dozen trembling seventh-grade girls gripped their violins, trying their utmost to avoid eye contact with the eighth-grade black girl who'd clearly staked out her territory. Perhaps it was because I'd grown bigger over the summer; whatever the reason, Dawnita had been distracted by the new mice.

I stayed scared of black girls for years. Loud voices, thick arms, laughs and slaps on the leg set my heart lurching and my white skin glistening with sweat. I'd turn and walk the other direction and if I had no choice, if I was forced to interact with one, I'd choose my words carefully and with purpose. Black girls anger easily, I thought. Black girls don't put up with white boys' jokes. Black girls hit hard.

But like most intelligent, contemplative people, I grew up and got over my Dawnita-induced racism, as evidenced by my genuine ease with the many people of color I encountered over the ensuing years. I say this with the utmost sincerity and perhaps some wishful thinking, because I want to believe wholeheartedly that I left my negative feelings regarding race at the doors of Port Gardner Middle School. I'm not naive, though. I know it's more complicated than that.

*   *   *

My partner Shayne and I bought our first house together in 1997, a Seattle saltbox-style duplex just down the hill from Garfield High School, alma mater of Jimi Hendrix and Quincy Jones; in fact, Quincy's childhood home was just around the corner from our building. When we moved in, the Central District of Seattle, known as the CD, had been in the midst of a transition, that inevitable happening that befalls most poor urban neighborhoods in which properties become a premium. It's the stereotype of a changing community: young couples, typically white, descend upon rundown bungalows and vacant lots and clean them up. The prices of the houses and the neighborhood's collective skin shade often rise in synchronicity with one another. Those longtime residents, often people of color (if the neighborhood is the African American section of town), usually seniors, become priced out of their own homes, unable to pay the rising taxes. And so they must sell. The new owners enjoy the charm of early twentieth-century architecture, the soul food restaurants, the respect of a community bound by history and shared experience. They love that they live in a racially diverse neighborhood, but the diversity of a culture that seems to draw in those eager, idealistic people is often not enough to sustain their progressive optimism. In fact, the unappetizing realities of urban culture quickly seep in, steeping them in disgust for the very reality they wind up actually experiencing.

It wasn't long before the sting of Dawnita's hand began to flavor my thoughts, my words, and my reactions. The tenant we displaced when we took occupancy of the duplex was a fierce woman—a black woman—dramatically outspoken, one moment sweet and jovial, the next furious at us for forcing her to move. Each time we discussed the process for moving her out, my stomach knotted and the fears of a twelve-year-old boy began to surface. In the end, we came to a mutual understanding. I recognized the sense of violation that we, these incoming, home-buying white guys, had created for her, and she acknowledged that we were seeking a permanent home for ourselves and that it was not a personal attack on her. All ended well, albeit a bit awkwardly, and I escaped without being beaten up.

As long as Shayne and I socialized with the neighbors, attended block watch meetings, and swapped stories with the longtime denizens of the neighborhood we felt welcome and safe. After all, we weren't the first white folks to have moved into the CD, and our work on the duplex had indeed been fueled by pride in the roots of the neighborhood as well as in the bones of our eighty-year-old home. Progressives that we were, we praised the unique feel of our neighborhood. The jovial conversations from parked car to doorstep, the friendly greetings from passersby as we kneeled in the garden pulling weeds, the echo of blues music from front porches in the still summer night air filled us with self-satisfaction. We were creating a new cycle of tolerance in the modern era. Gay and straight, black and white, together in a harmonious circle of life.

The fissures in this Pollyannaish world appeared soon enough. Two weeks after we moved in, gunshots rang out a few blocks away. Neither Shayne nor I reacted much, other than to raise our eyebrows and comment that it must be from Yessler Terrace, the subsidized housing project west of us, over the hill. No words were shared about who or what the shooter might look like; it was a given that it was probably a black gangbanger. The prostitutes working the corner of Jefferson and Twenty-Second just two blocks from us gave us little cause for concern.

"I don't have a problem with folks making a living," I'd say, wearing my streetwise attitude nonchalantly. Still, we didn't want to encourage the crack dealing that went hand in hand with selling sex, so we called the police whenever we passed by the women's beckoning hands.

Months went by; Shayne and I vacillated between loving our new home and cursing the space surrounding it. Condoms, needles, and general trash found its way into our garden on a regular basis. Any teenager walking down the sidewalk, jeans sagging past his thighs, cap pulled down over his eyes, was automatically suspect. Shiny sedans, windows tinted and rattling from subwoofer-pushed bass, idled for minutes in front of neighboring houses. We knew their occupants were dealing drugs. Two or more black teenagers gathered curbside enjoying a lively conversation that could be heard a block away was cause for us to monitor them, waiting for the crime that was surely about to happen.

We hated it. We hated the reality of urban life around us and, more important, we hated what we had allowed it to do to us. It was unspoken. We would never use epithets or even racial terminology, but the inclination to do so was there. "Baggy jean, do-rag wearin'" we'd mumble at our window, mocking rap music with, "Mother F. this and mother F. that" as the vibrating sedan rolled by our house. It allowed us to vent our frustration and disgust at a group of people without actually saying the words to make us racist. The distance we had created in our minds between "us" and "them" increased and the farther the distance, the higher we climbed and the lower they sank.

But at least their offenses were unabashed, right there in the open. Mine were hidden, unacknowledged, as they metastasized quietly beneath the surface. I didn't identify it then, but I understand now that it was the lyncher in me that swelled up, that there is a lyncher in each of us. We separate ourselves as superior, the other person growing less human with each act that rubs us the wrong way. Angry words lead to fantastic thoughts of revenge, violence, elimination. Logic pushes these away and with any luck, we grow more and more ashamed of what the experience has allowed us to become. We did; we weren't like this, like those hateful, ignorant racists. We were liberal, accepting people. We loved diversity, even lamenting the growing number of white-occupied houses around us. We wanted the color and the flavor without the unpleasant aftertaste.

We eventually moved from the city to a rural piece of land some distance away, though we still own the duplex as a rental. I'm glad that I can honestly say that it wasn't the issues described above that pushed us out, it was a simple desire for space and play room. We'd adopted a toddler and our duplex was near a busy street and not conducive to outside play. We return to the duplex often and each time we do, we lament the many things we miss about living there.

Over time, Shayne and I came to terms not just with the issues that angered us but with our guilt as well. We accepted that yes, each person has his or her own prejudices, buried deep beneath the various layers within. The right circumstances will bring those forward, and to deny the feelings is to deny reality. The responsible person grasps those feelings and digs down to expose the roots.

When we really sat down and contemplated what was happening in the CD, Shane and I realized that our discomfort wasn't about race at all, though that had been a convenient reaction. The desire for a safe, clean community isn't governed by color or ethnicity. Every resident on our street, black and white, turned out regularly to bag garbage, sweep the drive, and make sure one another's porch lights worked properly. It could be a white kid cranking a stereo up past our house, throwing trash into the planting strip, or shooting up next to our garage, and it would still anger us. We really had to own what was happening within us, because feelings don't cease to exist just because we say they don't exist. And saying we're above something is not too much different than standing on a pedestal.

After all, didn't we, the indignant new homeowners, have just as much gall, uptight white-bread boys tearing up ground that had once been used for walking and sticking in ornamental grasses, putting up fences and No Trespassing signs? Isn't that what white people do, descend on a neighborhood like vultures, raise the taxes so much that no long-timer can afford to live there, and call it a nice name like "gentrification"? Our frustrations didn't really have a color; assigning one was just an easy way of placing blame. In the end, it was about making the human connections with our community and understanding that we changed the composition of the neighborhood when we moved in, not the other way around. It was about assimilating, not taking over and I think that can be the hardest task of all.

My great-grandfather Louis Dondino, delivering for the Armour Company in Duluth, circa 1915

My great, great-grandparents Sarah and William's fiftieth wedding anniversary, August 9, 1914. They are seated in the second row, center, with the bouquet and lapel flower, respectively. My great-grandfather Louis is lying in the front row, second from the right. My grandfather Ray is the first child from the left, with the large necktie.

My grandfather Ray at the age of eleven or twelve (ca. 1918), with my great-great-grandmother Sarah

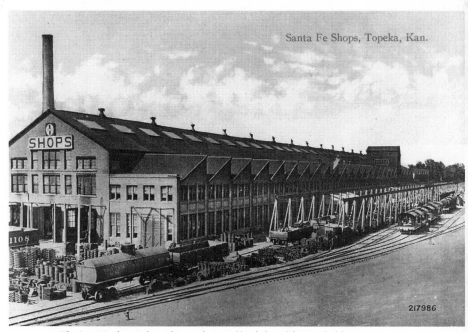

Santa Fe Shops, Topeka, Kan.

217986

The Santa Fe shops, where Elmer Jackson and his father Clifton worked from 1917 to 1919

The lynchings of Elmer Jackson, Elias Clayton, and Isaac McGhie, as captured by local photographer Ralph Greenspun. The photo would be sold as souvenir postcards in Duluth stores.

WILLIAM M. EMPIE, MAYOR

CITY OF VIRGINIA

MAYOR

Virginia, Minnesota
June - 19 - 1920.

Dear Tommie,

We got back and it is cold here. Many wearing overcoats. some relief from that weather down there.

We have had a lot of Excitement at Duluth, three negroes lynched,

am sending you the picture I spoke of.

In Haste.

W. M. E.

A letter from Virginia, Minnesota, mayor William M. Empie, in which he tells his friend of the lynchings four days earlier. "We have had a lot of excitement at Duluth," he writes, "three Negroes lynched."

My great-grandfather Louis (left)
and my grandfather Ray (right)
with their workhorse team, Buster
and Bob, in about 1946

My grandmother Margaret, my mother, and my grandfather Ray in 1950. My grandmother
always hated this photo, but my mother likes it: "I think it kind of shows what a ragamuffin
crew we were."

Louis Dondino, approximately 1950

Louis Dondino sometime around 1955, about two years before his death. He'd have been about seventy-five years old in this photo.

The Clayton, Jackson, McGhie Memorial viewed from the corner of Second Avenue East and First Street. The memorial is located diagonally opposite the corner where the lynchings took place.

Dick Green's House, Pennytown: taken in about 1900. The boy in front of the porch is Tom Jackson, cousin to Elmer Jackson.

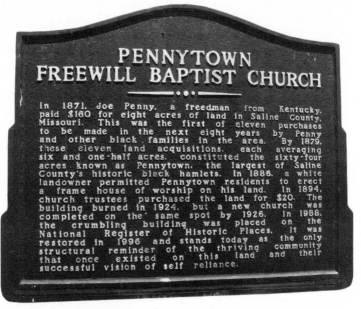

PENNYTOWN
FREEWILL BAPTIST CHURCH

In 1871, Joe Penny, a freedman from Kentucky, paid $160 for eight acres of land in Saline County, Missouri. This was the first of eleven purchases to be made in the next eight years by Penny and other black families in the area. By 1879, these eleven land acquisitions, each averaging six and one-half acres, constituted the sixty-four acres known as Pennytown, the largest of Saline County's historic black hamlets. In 1886, a white landowner permitted Pennytown residents to erect a frame house of worship on his land. In 1894, church trustees purchased the land for $20. The building burned in 1924, but a new church was completed on the same spot by 1926. In 1988, the crumbling building was placed on the National Register of Historic Places. It was restored in 1996 and stands today as the only structural reminder of the thriving community that once existed on this land and their successful vision of self reliance.

The plaque installed outside the Pennytown Church, telling the story of Joe Penny's monumental purchase in 1871

The Pennytown Freewill Baptist Church today

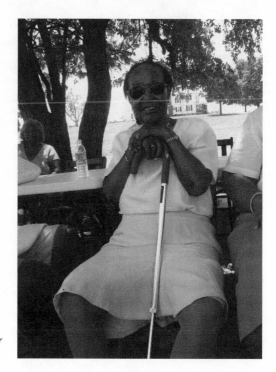

Mary Clariette Jackson, daughter of Tom Jackson, August 2006

Virginia Huston and me at the Pennytown reunion, August 2006

CHAPTER 21

 HE MINNESOTA HISTORICAL SOCIETY (MHS) has
amassed an exhaustive collection of documents, photos, and articles related to the Duluth lynchings. My great-grandfather's name comes up
ninety-six times in an MHS library search. Mostly they are letters from
his warden to his family, or receipts for monies sent from my great-
grandfather to his young son, my grandpa Ray. There are court documents and newspaper articles with his name mentioned. His personal biography is truncated and matter-of-fact:

> *Dondino, Louis (ca. 1882–)*
>
> *Louis Dondino was convicted of riot. Thirty-eight years old,*
> *Dondino was employed in Duluth as a truck driver. Hours before the*
> *lynchings he drove his truck through downtown Duluth, gathering*
> *men to join the mob. Witnesses also placed Dondino among the*
> *crowd of rioters.*
>
> *The crime of riot held a maximum sentence of five years. Dondino*
> *was paroled from prison in March 1922 and discharged a year later.*
> *He served about a year in Minnesota State Prison, Stillwater.*

An open-ended lifespan, a year of birth without a year of death. To
the casual reader, my great-grandfather died sometime between 1922
and the present date, the details of both his life and death unknown and
unimportant.

In actuality, Louis Dondino would live to be seventy-seven years old
and were it not for the remnants of bitterness and stubborn resistance
that I believe were fostered in his son in the aftermath of that night,
through the trials and the sentencing, my mother's grandfather might
have lived a bit longer.

By 1957, Louis had moved from a tiny shack adjacent to his son's family to a small house east of downtown Edmonds, off of the primary road
connecting Seattle to all towns north, Highway 99. A dirt road when

Louis had moved to the area in the late 1930s, Highway 99 had since begun sprouting a myriad of businesses along the increasingly busy street. A motel sat just to the north of Louis's place.

Earlier in the spring, Louis had contracted a strain of influenza and it had hit him hard, so much so that he'd been unable to take care of even his most basic needs; cleaning and feeding himself took much more energy than he had. At his age, Louis knew that the flu was not something to be taken lightly. My grandmother wholeheartedly agreed. She approached my grandfather to ask if she and my mother might stay with her father-in-law for a few days, at least until he was out of the woods. My grandpa Ray grumbled loudly, said he didn't see what the big deal was about, but in the end he reluctantly agreed to let them go.

Both my mother and her mother tended to Louis twenty-four hours a day, my grandmother staying with him during the day and my mother leaving his side only for school. Ray would come by in the evenings, after work, so that his wife could serve him dinner. After nearly two weeks, he concluded that his father was healthy enough, that it was time for his wife and daughter to come home. My grandmother disagreed, saying they'd "be better safe than sorry," but my grandfather simply put his foot down.

"I want you back home," he demanded. "He can take care of himself now." Louis didn't argue.

"I'll be fine," he reassured them.

For the first few days, my mother and grandmother called his house and he indeed seemed to be doing better. On the fourth day, though, Louis didn't answer his phone and for the next two days, it would be the same silence. Getting worried, my grandmother implored her husband to please go and check on him; my mother begged her father to let her take the school bus to his house to make sure he was all right.

"No, he's fine," he scolded. "You and your mother spent enough time over there; he can take care of himself!" He'd laid down the law and there wasn't to be another word said on the matter.

Several days later a man was walking along Highway 99, heading northward on the shoulder of the busy roadway. A faint noise, what sounded like a call for help, caught his ears. The man walked to the small house set back a bit from the road, next to the motel. Letting himself into the little shack, he discovered an old man lying in his bedroom, unable to move and nearly dead. From the looks of the invalid gentleman, of the condition of his bedclothes, it was obvious that he'd been there several days. At the hospital, the doctors diagnosed pleurisy, a painful inflammation of the membrane of his lungs, likely brought on by the pneumonia he'd developed since his family had left him alone.

"I remember it was during the week, so my dad said he couldn't take us to see him at the hospital until the weekend," my mother recalls. "I was beside myself and upset and scared he would die before we got there. Your grandma was worried, too, but it was no use trying to change the old man's mind."

That Saturday, the three of them finally made the fifteen-mile trip to the hospital, where Louis beamed, happy to see them at last. In the room, my mother stood on one side of the bed, my grandmother and grandfather on the other. Louis blinked his eyes and looked at his daughter-in-law.

"Nurse," he said to her, pointing at my grandfather, "this is my son."

"No, Pa, that's not the nurse," my mom corrected, "that's my mother," He looked away, confused, before mumbling, "Oh yeah."

"We're taking care of your dogs," my mother reassured him and he thanked her. While my grandmother held Louis's hand, Ray retreated from the bed, pacing along the wall, fidgeting and impatient. Finally, he announced that it was time to go. "Let him have his rest," he told them, and walked out of the room.

Nellie leaned over and kissed her Pa on the forehead, telling him they'd try and come back the next day to see him. "All right, sweetheart," he said.

That night the evening nurse from the hospital called; Louis had passed away shortly after they had left.

In her mind, both then and still today, my mother is screaming, furious at her father for allowing this to have happened. To this day she believes without a doubt that if he'd let them stay longer with her Pa the first time, or at least had gone to check on him in those days after Ray made his wife and daughter leave, her grandpa would still have been alive, that she'd have had a few more years with him. Maybe he'd have seen her through high school, been there for her in her young adult years. In the privacy of her room that night, she cursed her father, punched her pillow and grieved for the loss of the man who had been her one respite from the stifling embrace that was her home.

CHAPTER 22

On SEPTEMBER 11, 2001, I drove in the predawn darkness through the tiny waterside town of Kingston to the ferry. I was a new father, midway through my thirties, and this was a now-routine element of my long daily schedule: leave the house at 6:00 AM and sail across the waters of Puget Sound to the Edmonds ferry landing. From there, I'd walk through town to the side street on which I'd parked my "mainland car" and drive eastward through town to Interstate 5, then head north to my job as vice principal in Everett. Two hours from door to door each morning, even longer in the evenings coming home. To say that this complicated schedule was taking some adjusting to would be a gross understatement, but it was a choice I'd made, the price of living a rural lifestyle in suburban Seattle.

I listened to the crackling sound of a local radio station filtered through the bent antenna of my 1988 Corolla, the beater I'd purchased for the sole purpose of driving the three miles to and from the Kingston ferry. It was ten minutes at best, just enough time to hear the deejays riffing on the latest news, finding humor in celebrities' misfortunes. This morning, though, there had been something different in their routine; a concern in their voices that took the edge off the usual script. Something had happened in New York, they said. An airplane had crashed into one of the towers of the World Trade Center. The details were unclear, but it sounded to me like it might have been a small plane, maybe a single engine thing. I imagined there would be quite a few pictures to see online once I got to a computer.

By the time I boarded the ferry, the conversation around me clarified that this had been no single plane mishap. This was big, two jetliners, and there might be more coming. No one seemed to be making sense, but everyone was talking and as the horrific details streamed out over the news station as I drove to school it became painfully obvious that I would have a real crisis waiting for me once I arrived.

Nearly 50 percent of the students at my school were members of ethnic minority groups, 40 percent bilingual. A significant portion of these children were of Middle Eastern origin, Iraqi, specifically. I knew that when I walked through those doors, I was going to have to be ready for a variety of reactions: anger, confusion, helplessness. I'd need to be there for the staff, who would be looking to the administration to help them both process what was happening and somehow greet their students confidently and strongly. I'd need to have a plan in place for the children themselves, to help them understand the nature of the attacks and our geographic distance from where it was all taking place. Above all, the students would need to feel safe and understand that their neighbors, whom they would soon see resembled the men on the news, were not their enemies. And I'd have just over an hour to try to put all of this into place.

*　　*　　*

The adults in my family never really seemed willing to grasp hold of the overreaching elements that were eating away at our functionality, but we often show an uncanny ability to react to the challenge at hand, to operate with surprising deftness under urgent conditions. I think I learned this from my mother. I remember watching in awe as she shimmied into the crawlspace under an old woman's house to retrieve a stubborn housecat, simply because there was no one else around who would do it. And there was the night when my siblings and I became lost in the darkened labyrinth of a dilapidated barn, a claptrap, cut-rate Halloween haunted house. I wasn't more than five years old, but I can still hear her calling to us as she crawled her way toward the sounds of our voices. When we emerged with her into the night air, I noticed that she was wearing only one shoe; the other had been lost when her foot broke through the rotted floorboards somewhere along the way. Act now, worry later, was the lesson I'd learned from her. She's always been the kind of person who just accepts what has been placed in front of her and deals with it.

In actuality, I think that my mother thrives on crisis; when there is no drama in her life, she tends to get bored. When the flames flare up, she switches into problem-solving mode, taking care of the situation as she thinks best. Perhaps that's why she's successfully worked her way up the rungs of the state social-services ladder, deservedly holding a supervisory position and putting out fires daily. She often will call me at the end of a long week, exhausted and sometimes frustrated with the nonstop activity of the previous days. But I know she'd have it no other way. A story she's shared with me on many an occasion (and one I love to hear) is a perfect example of my mother at her survival-mode best. It's a tale of danger, snap judgments, and just the right amount of naiveté to ensure a surprise ending.

*   *   *

July of 1968 had been shaping up to be a hot one, both meteorologically and socially, as anyone who lived through that summer can attest. Seattle hadn't had a day's high temperature stop short of eighty (which, for Seattleites, is a heat wave). The newspapers of the time report a series of lake and river drownings, one after the other, as locals took to the water to enjoy the rarity of a sweltering day. (This unfortunate side effect of good weather is still prevalent today.)

Culturally and politically, the summer of '68 was also sizzling. Confusion and hopelessness seemed to grip the nation as its people wrestled with the chaos of Vietnam, the brutal killings of Martin Luther King Jr. just four months earlier and, most recently, the assassination Bobby Kennedy. And as if things weren't crazy enough, my parents were confronted with the fact that two of my sisters were missing.

I was just over a year old, a chubby toddler stumbling around our rental house at Lake Stickney, just north of Seattle. Several weeks before, my sisters Julie and Beth had gone to California with their biological mother, Linda, for what was to be an extended visit. Linda's trustworthiness as a mother hadn't been stable up until then—she was young (barely out of her teens), worked as a go-go dancer, drank heavily, and surrounded herself with the same caliber of people—but her recent behavior suggested that she had left those behaviors behind, that she might be ready to take on more parental responsibilities. And so the plan had been for her to return the girls within a few weeks, but that didn't happen. Linda didn't contact my parents and they had no working phone number for her. Days went by and with no word on the girls, both my mother and father had begun worry. While it had seemed that my father's ex-wife had pulled herself together enough to have the girls for a short time, the fact that she'd simply disappeared was more than enough to set alarms ringing.

"Linda had told us that she was remarried to a merchant seaman and she promised to make sure the girls got dental work and new clothes for school," she explains. "So we thought it was safe to send them to her, since we had custody. Of course we learned later that meant nothing when the kids were in another state." To further complicate things, they'd later find out that Linda wasn't married at all, but had in fact been working as a go-go dancer and a stripper the entire time.

Out of the blue, a letter finally arrived for my father, with a return address in Los Angeles. It was from Linda, telling my father, "Come and get them."

"She was broke," my mother says, "so if we wanted the girls back, your father was going to have to either send money or go there himself." My father had a job he couldn't leave and my parents couldn't afford the loss of income anyway, so the burden fell on my mother to make the trip. She was twenty-four years old, and she had never even been out of the Seattle area, much less Washington State.

But none of that really mattered in the end. "It had to be done, and I didn't have time to be scared," she says. "Someone had to take responsibility for them and there sure as hell weren't people coming out of the woodwork to do it." And so she went.

My mother packed a small suitcase and boarded a Greyhound bus headed for Los Angeles, with the envelope's return address as a guide. "When you get there," my father had told her, "call my uncle who lives in L.A. He's in the phone book. His name is George Martin." My mother laughs today at this last sentence, though it had to have been far from funny as she stood in the overwhelming chaos of the downtown Los Angeles bus depot.

"Do you know how many phone books there were for Los Angeles, even then?" she asks incredulously. "I couldn't even narrow it down to the right section or neighborhood or whatever you call those parts of town. And don't even get me started on the number of George Martins I found in the books."

With a little help from a bystander, she was able to locate a bus route that dropped her near the address on the envelope, which was in what she describes as a "very diverse neighborhood, not poor-looking, but many different nationalities." She walked along the sidewalk to a large, two-story apartment complex. Finding the right apartment, she could see that it was empty and she wandered through the complex's courtyard, knocking on doors until she finally located the manager's unit on the ground floor.

"I remember he was a somewhat overweight white guy with an Asian wife or girlfriend, and she stayed in the background and didn't say anything the whole time I was there." She told the couple why she'd come to Los Angeles and the man rolled his eyes knowingly.

"Oh, they left," he said. "I felt so sorry for those poor kids, always in that apartment with the drapes closed, even in this damned heat." He went on to explain that Linda and her boyfriend Clarence had lived there, that they'd "fought all the time, day and night." It had been about two weeks previously that it had come to a head, when Linda, it a fit of rage, took a straight razor to all of Clarence's clothes, throwing them out the apartment door and into the courtyard. "I had to kick her out after that, you know. We just can't have that kind of thing happening here."

"I told him that I was there to get the kids and that if I didn't find them, I'd be calling the police," she says. "This was a bluff, of course." At this, my mother leans forward, almost like she's still shielding this secret weapon. "I had already found out that the cops wouldn't do a damned thing and that we'd have to hire a lawyer in California if she didn't give them up—which we didn't have the money for. As it was, we'd had to borrow two hundred dollars from Household Finance (a finance company for the poor and/or desperate that charged 25 percent interest) to go in the first place." The manager pulled a small spiral notebook from beneath a stack of papers, spun some numbers on the rotary phone, and waited a few seconds before speaking.

"Yeah, you'd better get over here," he told the person on the other end. "This girl's here to get Linda's kids and if she can't find them, she's gonna call the cops."

*   *   *

Within a half hour, a huge red and white sedan screeched to a stop outside the apartment; a tall, stocky black man sauntered out. "He had a couple of rings and a gold chain, I remember. He was dressed smoothly, all in black with just a bit of gold trim along the collar of his shirt." She fingers the neckline of her blouse and I laugh. "Hey," she says defensively, "it was the sixties, man."

Clarence nervously approached her—this towering black man facing off against a terrified young white woman who was lying desperately through her teeth—and told her that he'd take her to where the girls were. "I can't say she'll give them to you," he said, "but I'll take you there." And so my mother climbed into this stranger's car and they drove off, to a section of Los Angeles that my mother would later find out was known as Watts.

"I still cringe when I think about it. Here I'm making this threat to go to the cops and when this man I don't even know agrees to take me, I just hop into his car like, 'yeah, sure, whatever'. . ." She's amused with her youthful ignorance now. "I was so stupid and naive; I could have wound up on the show *Cold Case Files*."

They came to a stop in front of a large house, rustic and unpainted, an expansive covered porch fronting the structure. "A black woman, probably in her mid-fifties, was standing on the front steps. She didn't seem at all surprised to see us there." The woman called for Linda, who stomped angrily to the porch, screaming at Clarence for having brought my mother. "When she came out yelling," my mother recalls, "Clarence just disappeared. He was there next to me one second and then he was gone. He turned tail and jumped back into the car and laid rubber all the way down the block."

Linda marched back into the house, followed by the older woman, then my mother. "The curtains were drawn partway and the room was dark and musty and looked like it might be a boarding house of some kind," she says. I ask her what gave her that impression and she shrugs her shoulders. "I don't know, really. There was furniture, but it was sparse and cheap. It was tidy, but in a way that seemed like the room was never used, and there were doors open down the hallway that I thought probably had people in them."

"It's better that you take the kids home," the woman said quietly to my mother. "That's all I want to do," she replied.

Linda called out from one of the back bedrooms, "I know you're going to tell their father that I'm living with black people and there's nothing wrong with that!" she yelled.

"Linda, it doesn't matter, we don't care," my mother answered in a deliberately calm, cool voice. "And meanwhile," she says now, "I can hear scurrying and noise all around me and I knew there were other people there, but I couldn't see them. It was really pretty creepy." It was as if the commotion was stirring up the formerly dormant residents and the more volatile Linda became, the more my mother began to fear for her safety. She knew she had to get out quickly.

"The girls came out," she recalls. "They had their hair in little braids all over their heads. They were hanging on to my leg and I remember Beth asking how the pony was (we had a Shetland pony that we kept in a pasture behind our rented house) and both girls were saying they wanted to go home."

Linda reappeared in the living room, dragging a large, stained cardboard box filled with the girls' clothes. "Go, just go!" she yelled and my mother, not needing to be told twice, left and made her way down the sidewalk with the box in one hand and the hands of two crying girls in the other. As they turned the corner at the end of the block, she stopped and rifled through the box. "I saw that the clothes were all dirty and they smelled bad, so I drug it into an alley and left it there."

Another bus took them to the station where she led the girls into a small shop, the kind that sold items ranging from shoes to motor oil. "I bought some shorts outfits for the girls, a red-checked shirt for me. We took a shower for a quarter and when I brought them to the café to get something to eat, Beth said, 'I want candy,' and I said, 'We're having chili.' We were sitting there and I guess we looked like a little family because this guy who was nearby looking at us says, 'They your daughters?' and I said 'Yeah,' and he says, 'They look like you.' And all the while I'm thinking, 'Yeah right. Jesus H. Christ if you only knew.'"

I am filled with overwhelming admiration for my mother every time I hear this story. To be twenty-four years old, a virgin traveler outside of her own backyard, and agree to take on such a daunting journey with no hesitation is truly heroic in my eyes. I'm not sure I'd have had it in me to do it. It reminds me that, in spite of the fact that we don't always make the best choices in my family, it's not in our natures to stand by idly and do nothing. And that's a priceless trait I've learned from her. Don't wait around for someone else to take charge because by the time they do, it might be too late.

*　　*　　*

September 11, 2001. We stood in front of a wall-sized map of the United States there in the cafeteria of our school, the guidance counselor and I, speaking with the students. My finger traced a line from New York to Washington State and we counted in unison the number of states we passed on the way. We discussed the scary things they would probably see on the news and that the crashes they saw would be the same ones being shown over and over, not many crashes into many different buildings. They would hear ugly things being said about people, people who would look a lot like their neighbors and their classmates. They'd hear talk about Arabs and Muslims and we wanted them to understand that these were not bad words but good words that might be used in a bad way. We increased supervision that week, not due to any fear of our Iraqi community but to protect against any hysterical reactions by others. And in spite of the incredible horrors that continued to unfold that day and in the coming days, I can say without hesitation that things ran unbelievably smoothly within the little world that was our school.

In hindsight, were there things that could have been done better? Certainly. But when confronted with a situation that needs an immediate action, we take what are our most basic impulses and hope that they are coming from a foundation of solid character and sound principles. And so with the Clayton, Jackson, McGhie Memorial, I was faced with the unthinkable and gifted with the possibility of making a terrible wrong somehow right. I knew that to be passively unresponsive was not an option. Sure, it would be excruciating to fully confront my family's role in the lynching; what we'd learned already hurt terribly. Even more so, it might be absolutely humiliating to travel to Duluth and face it in person. But both my mother and I agreed that we had no choice but to step up and do it. I suppose it was our very natures that vaulted us ahead without overthinking it, sailing us forward to worry later about where and how we might land.

CHAPTER 23

CATHERINE OSTOS of the Clayton Jackson McGhie Memorial Committee contacted me in the spring of 2003, about a year after we'd first spoken. The memorial was to be completed and dedicated the following October, she explained, and the committee hoped that I would be willing to be a keynote speaker at the ceremony. They felt that mine would be an important voice, a connection between the tragedy of 1920 and the healing of 2003. "It would mean so much, it would be the perfect contribution to the memorial," she said.

And so I agreed, offered myself up before I'd even had a chance to really process the implications of her request. I'd spoken in public before, so the idea of addressing a large group of people didn't faze me. "How hard could it be?" I thought. "Talk for a few minutes to a few hundred people at most. I've done that before." I spent many nights over the next six months scribbling, crossing out, second-guessing, and crafting a speech that would say both what I wanted to say and what I thought the community of Duluth would want to hear. I'd be speaking for not just my family, but the families of every person who had been present that night; the men in the photo, caught forever, and the thousands hiding safely beyond its frame. It was an undertaking that, thankfully, I didn't think about too deeply before accepting.

I live on the peninsula of Washington State, across the great body of water called Puget Sound from Seattle. There are three ways to get from my house to the city: the ferry system, the Tacoma Narrows Bridge south of Seattle, and the incredibly long route via Olympia, all the way to the bottom of the scoop of the Sound. The morning of my flight to Duluth, we'd opted to drive south across the bridge to Tacoma, then double back up to Sea-Tac airport. Unfortunately, there had been an accident on the bridge (as tends to happen whenever a rainstorm hits the city) and by the time we were in the thick of the traffic backup, there was no choice but to wait it out. Turning around and taking an alternate route would be an additional three-hour trip, at minimum.

Shayne and I sat in the car, wedged between immovable vehicles, brake lights glaring in front and headlights beaming through the rearview mirror. I compulsively checked my watch every few minutes, craning my neck out the window, hoping to see some movement up ahead.

"I don't think we're going to make it," said Shayne. "This traffic isn't going anywhere."

I scratched my scalp, itchy from the perspiration that was coming with rattled nerves. I tried to sound optimistic. "It might clear out just around this corner." We rolled slowly ahead, then stopped again. The drone of the radio amplified my anxiety and I switched it off. "Come on!" I growled. The rain drummed the rooftop, a pounding reinforcement of what Shayne had already concluded. I hated the rain. I hated the lousy drivers who had succumbed to it, ignoring the slickness of the road and racing to wherever they'd been going. The noise, the sense of being trapped, was nearly pushing me over the edge.

Outside, sheets of water flowed from the center of the road into the gutters. A light sheen of color danced on the surface, the remnants of petroleum and filth washing into the hapless soil. I rolled down the window and breathed in the stale, dank odor of a fresh urban cleaning.

"I love the smell that comes right after a new rainstorm," Shayne said.

"Yeah," I agreed, and I do. Even though it's not something I'd want piped into my house or wafting from an incense stick, there's definitely something about the smell of rain that is calming to the brain, and I tried to go with it. Maybe it's that sense of renewal, I told myself, wiping clean last month's dirt to make room for the new. I could understand why it's so deceptive to the hurried driver or the pedestrian with his new leather-soled shoes, each distracted and caught unaware of the glare of sunlight bouncing off the roadway and the thin layer of silt on its surface. With cleansing can come a dangerous residue, I thought. By speaking at the memorial, I would be washing filth from my family, but at what risk? Poisoning the soil? Tripping up innocent bystanders?

I was being ridiculous, overanalyzing as usual. It was a rainstorm. A downpour in Seattle, and I was trying to make a Fellini film out of it.

We crossed the bridge, the traffic opening up at last, and we moved at a quick clip toward the airport. The rain had finally let up and the only job for my wipers was clearing the spray from the windshield. We pulled into the parking garage twenty minutes before my plane's departure time, and regardless of my willingness to run all the way to the gate, I was too late. I wouldn't make the flight and as a consequence, I'd miss that evening's committee meeting in Duluth, the final one before the memorial unveiling. I'd really wanted this, to sit down with the people behind this huge undertaking, meet them outside of the frenetic activity that was waiting for us all the next day. As it was, I wouldn't have the smooth transition that I'd hoped for nor have any time to get my bearings in a strange city. Thankfully, I was able to secure a flight later in the day. I still had just under twenty-four hours until the memorial unveiling; as long as there wasn't a sudden October blizzard in Minneapolis, I knew I'd be fine.

When I finally arrived in Duluth, I was met by a beautiful young woman waving enthusiastically at me, her smile radiantly greeting me as I fished for my luggage on the carousel. It was Catherine Nachbar, one of the members of the memorial committee. I was relieved to see her, since I'd not been able to contact anyone to tell them I'd missed my flight and I wasn't sure anyone would know where I was (I race to get to destinations on time, I don't always prepare for an unexpected event by bringing peoples' phone numbers). Catherine explained that she knew I'd be late, that a television reporter had contacted the committee to tell them of my missed flight. Apparently, this woman had called the airline to see when I'd be arriving in Duluth and the ticket agent had explained that a car accident had kept me from my scheduled departure, but that I'd boarded the next one. This was translated in Catherine's mind that it had been *me* who had crashed my car and she was naturally relieved to see me walking out in one piece. On the way to her car, she filled me in on what I'd missed at the meeting earlier, the itinerary for the next day, and the committee's hope that thousands of people would turn out for the ceremony. We came up over a slight hill and the low buildings of downtown Duluth rose into view.

"Do you want to see the jail?" she asked suddenly.

"Sure," I said, and she exited the freeway and drove into the deserted city streets. We turned a corner and drove to the end of the block, pulling alongside the building. It looked almost the same as I remembered it from the snapshot of the battered jailhouse in Michael Fedo's book. Its scrubbed brick face gleamed red even under the dim glow of the evening streetlamp. Minus the screaming masses and the grainy atmosphere of the photo, it was certainly a less ominous place. The attorneys' sign across the window softened its harsh notoriety; a passerby not up on his history would probably walk by without a second look, except to glance at his own reflection, brush his hair to the side.

"The monument's right up here," she said as we pulled away. Turning left up the hill we came to a stop at the curb and got out of the car. "That's the corner there," she said softly, pointing to a tall blue lamppost that shone an apron upon the entire corner, a spotlight illuminating emptiness.

I turned to the opposite corner. Ghostly figures, three of them, loomed several feet above the ground. They stood with authority, with regal prominence amid the gleaming pale walls that framed the corner lot. As I approached, I soaked in the words that had been beautifully carved in the stone surround: "An event has happened upon which it is difficult to speak and impossible to remain silent." Loud rock music and drunken laughter spilled out of The Kozy Bar just across the street. I laughed at the odd connection.

"We have a Kozy Tavern in Everett," I told Catherine, the memory of one of Lenny's favorite haunts drifting back to me with the noise. "And it's just as classy, I have to say."

*   *   *

The first time Lenny took me to The Kozy, it had been surprisingly familiar. An invitation to accompany him on a ride with a friend had seemed
harmless enough. "Cool," I thought. "Run some errands—I might get a
Coke or even a milkshake out of it." The three of us squeezed into the cab
of Lenny's tiny pickup truck; Bob, round and wheezing, rode shotgun
and my eleven-year-old self was crammed in the middle, shoulders and
thighs pressed in a human vice as we headed up the freeway into the
north end of Everett. Just a couple of stops, one at a hardware store and
the other at Al's Auto Parts, and we were off again, heading back down
Broadway, left at Hewitt. Suddenly the truck lurched to the right and
pulled alongside the curb in front of a tavern. The neon beer signs cast
a blue glow into the cab of our pickup and I looked nervously over at
Lenny. My gut gave a foreboding roll as I began to realize what was about
to happen.

"We'll be right back," Lenny assured me as he and Bob jumped out of
the cab and slammed the door behind them. I sat obediently, squinting
through the red loop of the Rainier logo and anticipating the Coke I
prayed would be coming out with them any minute.

An hour later, I sat in the truck, crying, swearing at Lenny that I knew
goddamned good and well what was going on. I'd heard the stories from
my mom about what men who drank did to their kids.

*   *   *

When my grandparents were on the road, passing by a tavern was an exercise in impromptu prayer for my grandmother, hoping that the car
would continue past the parking lot. Too often, my grandfather would
turn the steering wheel and pull into a spot out back, bringing the car to
rest in a cloud of dust.

"Wait here, I'll be right back," he'd promise, leaving my grandmother
and my mother to wait in the car. My grandmother might begin a feeble protest and he'd simply brush her off. "I'm just gonna get a couple a'
beers," he'd promise. Turning to his daughter, he'd typically offer, "How
about a Hershey bar and a 7-Up for you? No Coke—it's bad for ya!"

Sometimes my grandmother would plead more loudly. "Ray," she'd
say, "I gotta get home and set the rolls up for tomorrow!"

"Yeah, yeah, just a couple a' beers. I ain't gonna be long!"

Defeated, my grandmother Margaret's shoulders would drop helplessly. "Dadgummit, I knew he'd do this!" She'd sit quietly, just a faint whisper of a cry under her breath. If my mother began to get fidgety and start to whine, her mother would be spurred into denial mode.

"Oh well," she'd tell her daughter, "he'll be back in a minute with the pop. Now don't you say anything to him!"

They might sit for three hours in the car, sometimes even longer. Since my grandmother would neither leave her daughter alone nor so much as darken the doorstep of a tavern, her husband knew he was perfectly safe from his wife's pious meddling.

In the car, Margaret and Nellie would entertain themselves with rounds of I Spy or word games using nearby signs. "How many words can you make out of 'tavern'?" "Rat, vat . . ."

If the stay went into the night, Margaret sang songs with her daughter.

I see the moon, and the moon sees me!
God bless the moon, and God bless me!

*   *   *

I stood outside the Kozy Tavern in Everett, just to the right of the door, snapping to attention when another drunken patron sauntered out. An occasional riot of laughter or colorful four-letter word would give me a start and I'd cup my hands to the tinted windows, peering inside to get a peek at what was happening. Several times, a new customer would pass by me and swing the door open, letting out a waft of smoke and chatter, like air escaping from the stem of a tire. Once a woman said "Hiya, sweetie," and a man, an old man who looked as if this tavern had been the last stop in a busy night, shuffled past me and complimented me for "holding up the building real good."

I may as well have been invisible otherwise. People came in and out, more or less ignoring me and certainly not taking the time to find out why I was standing outside the Kozy Tavern at 10:30 PM. In all likelihood, they knew. Maybe they'd been in my shoes once upon a time and hadn't the nerve to let me know that I'd probably be better off if I just went back to the truck and got comfortable. I slid down the wall, planting my rear on the cold sidewalk and resting my head on my arms. The pool of spit that I was making out of sheer boredom had grown to the size of a baseball by the time Bob emerged through doors. Pulling his belt up to his belly, he looked down at me with absolutely no surprise or remorse whatsoever.

"Lenny's coming out in a minute," he said. "He's pretty drunk."

The ride home was miserable. Lenny slumped in the middle, in and out of consciousness, going back and forth between mutterings of "You're my partner, aren't you?" and "You're just a fat little mama's boy." Pinched between his middle and forefinger, the glow of his lit cigarette waved uncomfortably close to my bare arm and I squeezed closer to the door, hoping he wouldn't notice, but in some part wishing that he'd just get it over with and burn me, so that I could stop worrying about it and start thinking of the nifty injury I'd have to show my mother. It wouldn't matter that the burn had been unintentional. By the time we got home, I'd make sure that that was it, the final straw that would send him packing once and for all. After all, I'd heard the stories—the hours upon hours that my mother had been left waiting while her father closed down the tavern. The last thing she would tolerate was a man pulling the same insanity on her own son.

The next morning, my mother came into my room to wake me up. Sitting on the edge of my bed, she ran her hand through my hair and sighed. "I talked with him about it," she told me. "He said it won't happen again."

My heart sank as I realized that Lenny's grip was quite possibly unbreakable. And when he saw me next, just a couple hours later, not a word was uttered to me about the previous night, not "sorry," not even an "oops!" It was as if the whole thing had never happened. I learned pretty quickly that when it came to Lenny, nothing ever really happened. He would call me names, hit me or drag me out of bed while he was in a drunken stupor; it never happened. I'd be punished for not organizing the truckload of car parts and cinder blocks he'd brought home in the middle of the night and in spite of the sheer insanity of it all, nothing really happened. He'd apologize to my mother, she'd relay the message to me, and things would be par for the course when I next saw him. No responsibility, no acknowledgment whatsoever to me. I was just supposed to know that he regretted what he'd done.

*   *   *

It's an odd feeling, revisiting the site of an old wound so many years after the injury. Age, experience, and wisdom are supposed to strengthen us, make us impervious to the pain. But as I stood there in downtown Duluth, the neon beer signs buzzing, the uncanny parallels between this spot and the Kozy Tavern of my childhood memory floated to the surface along with that eleven-year-old boy's anger.

The roar of singing and shouting spilled from the suddenly opened door and Catherine laughed and rolled her eyes. "I think there's probably a Kozy in every town," she said. "We're hoping that our next purchase is that spot," she nodded her head toward the tavern. She talked about the committee's ongoing dream of making that intersection a place of contemplation, expanding the memorial to maybe include a learning center of some kind, a way of addressing issues of racism that, she felt, had gone unmentioned for too long in Duluth.

"Yeah," I said. "It would be a much better use of space than what it's being used for now."

*   *   *

The sun shining through the blinds woke me up before the alarm had a chance to. I lay there under the covers in Catherine and her husband Jay's guest room, going over in my head what I'd dreamed the night before.

We'd been marching to the memorial, me in front with Catherine and a group of men and women I didn't know, people who kept turning to look at me. My mother had been next to me too, and she was crying. She was embarrassed, she'd said, afraid the people would find out who she was.

As we climbed over the hill—in my dream, it was a massive incline—the memorial came into view. But instead of the wall and the bronze relief I'd seen the night before, there loomed at the crest three silhouettes, dark and rail-thin, stretched into a grotesque likeness of human beings.

125

They stood alone, commanding the barren hilltop, and I was terrified to go any further. "It's okay," Catherine had said and when I turned to my mother, she'd gone, nowhere to be seen.

*   *   *

On the way to breakfast, I told Catherine about my dream.

"What do you think it means?" I asked, sarcastically predicting impending doom.

"It means it's all going to be okay," she reassured. Just like she'd said in the dream. "It's okay."

We climbed out of the car and I shifted under the weight of my sports jacket, glancing up at the sky for reassurance that the promised rain had indeed stood us up. A cloudless expanse mixed dreamily with the aroma of roasted coffee beans and my mouth watered at the thought of the hearty breakfast awaiting me. The café was one of those groovy, eclectic places with organic fruits and eggs, whole-grain granola and deep, wonderfully strong java. Catherine Ostos met me as I walked in, greeting me with a hearty hug—one of those you-let-go-first kind of embraces where I feel guilty for being the first to break away. The top of her head just reached my chest, but she may as well been ten feet tall as far as I was concerned. She was in command of the day, we had a lot waiting for us in the hours ahead and when she pulled away at last, her radiant smile showed me that she would make sure I was safe and comfortable for the rest of the trip.

"Thank you so much for being here," she said. "I wasn't sure you were going to make it when I heard about the accident." Chicago. I can't always pinpoint dialects, but Chicago I know.

As we ate whole-grain pancakes, she outlined the day for me. We'd be gathering at the waterfront park, she explained, and leave from there to walk to the memorial. We'd be walking the same route through town that the mob had taken eight decades earlier.

"We hope to get close to as many people as were there that night," she said. "We want to counter that crowd with one of our own." She also explained that I'd be "swarmed" when I got to the park, that reporters had been chomping to see me since the committee had announced that

I'd be the keynote speaker. "There are a lot of people who want to talk with you."

As the crowd began to build around the starting point, I pulled away to talk with a couple of newspaper and magazine writers and answer a few short questions for a local television field reporter. Just as I was walking to the gathered marchers to try to locate my two Catherines, a young man ran up, thrusting a cell phone toward me. A National Public Radio affiliate wanted a few, final moments of my time.

There were at least two thousand people between where I stood and where I needed to be but breaking free to make my way to the front was proving to be nearly impossible. The NPR reporter had asked why I'd come to Duluth that day, and I thought about why on earth I felt it was so important for me to travel so far to be here for this ceremony. I'd considered the question before I was handed the phone, but there had been a delay in the audio that was throwing me off; I'd pause after a short answer and when there was no response, I'd continue on. More than once, we stepped right over the top of one another clumsily and about the third time it happened, I'd laughed nervously. Immediately I felt horrible at the inappropriateness of the moment. Me, making light and actually laughing at the topic of murder, mutilation, and atonement for a family's sins. I told myself that I must have sounded like a complete idiot; I wouldn't have been surprised if the NPR station disconnected the call right then and there. The reporter asked if I'd seen the memorial yet and I replied that I had; when he pressed me for my impression of it, I told him that I thought it was "absolutely beautiful," that the committee "should be very proud of itself." Then my voice choked and I swallowed reflexively; for a brief moment it chased away my embarrassment at my strange laughter earlier. Ending the conversation with a more somber and genuine show of emotion was the best thing that could have happened. I flipped the cell phone closed.

I wove my way through the huge crowd, eyes focused on the front of the procession. The sun's heat coupled with my slow jog though the crowd had me pulling eagerly at my collar and wishing I could have left my tie (and about twenty pounds) with my jacket in the car. There were others leading the march, many would also be speaking to the crowd very soon. I wondered what these people I brushed past, these revelers who politely let me by with not so much as a glance my way, would think about me when I looked them in the eyes and exposed my ugly secret to them.

Catherine Nachbar took my arm like the perfect escort she'd been the whole trip and pointed out the rest of the committee members in front of me. Catherine Ostos and Henry Banks, the leaders of the amazing effort behind both the memorial to the three murdered men and the celebration today, marched at the front, leading a crowd whose intentions were in stark contrast to that of the mob eighty years ago on this same route.

We turned right and headed down Superior Street; the refurbished office buildings that had once been a busy collection of hotels, cafes, and clothing stores towered on both sides, gracing us with a merciful gift of shade. I opened a midlevel shirt button and waved my shirt in and out, breathing a sigh of relief at the cool air soothing my stomach and chest. Behind me a mass of moving bodies smiled, sang, and waved to the on-lookers who peered from office windows and sidewalks in wonder and curiosity. Some on the sidelines waved back, shouting words that I took as encouraging. Others seemed confused and unaware of the origin and purpose of this grand parade. The jovial music of the New Orleans Tremé Brass Band swam overhead and drifted back and as far as my eyes could see, the outstretched arms that came together in concert with the rhythms told me that the experience at the back was not much different from my own. Bouncing bodies, hands dancing in jubilation—as long as the parallels weren't drawn too carefully, as long as I kept my mind in the present century, it was truly a celebration.

Catherine N. reached over, squeezed my arm, and said something I couldn't hear as she pointed ahead. I glanced to my right and smiled back at the *St. Paul Pioneer Press* reporter with whom I'd spoken earlier. He nodded and scratched a few notes on his pad.

The procession ground to a halt as the Tremé Brass Band grew suddenly silent; I realized what Catherine had been calling my attention to. It was the jail, and what a difference daylight and a crowd of thousands made. A funeral march swelled, music so heavy and laden with sincerity it demanded reverence, contemplation. And I embraced, for the first time, the significance of this spot, my place on this hallowed ground. My heart broke. In front of me I saw the men, those helpless boys kicked, beaten, and dragged unmercifully as their pleas for justice fell on deaf ears. And I felt the pull—from eighty-three years away I felt the powerful pull of the mob, and its ugliness was overwhelming.

Common threads spanned the decades, holding them firmly together like clasped hands on this warm, glorious day. Three black men in the beginnings of their young lives, falsely accused of a crime unforgivable, dragged to their deaths in the most humiliating and voyeuristic manner. And me, my bloodline reaching back through generations as I stood where my ancestor stood hurling epithets and bricks on that fateful night. I stared at the old jailhouse, studying the columned doorway, the arched windows, the narrow sidewalk leading to the rear of the building where the mob at last broke through before descending upon the young men who lay crouched and terrified in their cells. I imagined the sobbing, their pleading, their defiant last walk as they were led to their own murder. And I pictured my great-grandfather in my place, gazing at the jail just as I was, only sneering, shouting encouragement to "get the niggers," struggling to help control the fire hose as it blasted the police officers off of their feet. The images were unrelenting. I felt my stomach sink, my throat swelled unexpectedly, and tears ran down my face as I wept for the shame I felt toward my family, for the remorse that I had to believe that my great-grandfather eventually felt and, most importantly, for the unspeakable horror that Elmer Jackson, Isaac McGhie, and Elias Clayton surely felt that night as they walked the very path I was about to complete.

"If I'm like this here," I called to Catherine, "How will I possibly make it through an entire speech?"

As it turned out, there was much time for me to collect myself. Many people had much to say, the mayor, author Michael Fedo, a state supreme court judge, and members of the memorial committee. Two hours later, almost all of those who had marched the route remained, staring intently as I approached the podium.

I hadn't even tried to imagine how the audience would react to my being there. As Catherine Ostos would later tell me, she'd wondered what I could possibly say to these thousands of people. As I'd sat at my desk, struggling to put words to paper, I felt a triad of responsibility—to say what I wanted to say, to express what my mother wanted to say about her grandfather, and (most difficult to predict) to say something the community of Duluth would want to hear. Above all, I knew that I had to do the one thing that I'd always wanted from everyone else in my life: drop the denials and excuses and take responsibility—as a man, as a family member, as a member of humanity.

I also felt compelled to give a clearer picture of my great-grandfather, "for the sake of helping to more fully tie 1920 to the present day," as I put it in my speech. I told them that I thought that one of the things that added to a sense "of being trapped within the horrible postcard of that night" was that it had for so long existed in a snapshot. "People involved are viewed in a singular dimension," I said. "By bringing it to the present, adding details and new eyes to this very location we can seek to balance the horror with a sense of pathos, dignity, and healing."

And so I told them about the gentle man named Louis, I gave them the story of Black Bill and the unwavering friendship that Louis had with him. I explained that we had no idea whether or not Louis felt remorse for his role in the lynching, but that we had to believe "that the way in which he completed his life, the example that he was for his granddaughter and his friends later in life spoke this for him."

I spoke of humility, and the wonderful opportunity for learning that this day held. And I explained my feelings about taking responsibility, and that I felt it was imperative that my great-grandfather do just that. But since he clearly couldn't be there in person to voice his feelings, I stood as a "representative of his legacy," and in doing so, I placed that responsibility on my shoulders.

And I apologized, on behalf of my family, each victim receiving his own acknowledgment.

"For Elmer Jackson," I said, "I am sorry that unreason and bigotry disallowed you the right to prove your innocence and deprived you the opportunity to create a legacy of your choosing.

"For Elias Clayton. Ignorance and self-righteousness were the fuel for your untimely and undignified death. For this, I offer my deepest apologies.

"For Isaac McGhie. I give you my heartfelt apology. Fear can never be used as an excuse for hysteria and passage of time can never be used as a reason for ignoring an injustice."

I vowed that, at least in my own family, the memories of that night and the current day would be forever valued and utilized as a teaching tool for tolerance, acceptance, and humility.

The crowd was ecstatic. As I returned to my seat, Catherine O. stood and embraced me in that commanding, genuine way she has, saying, "That was wonderful." One after another, people came up to me—men, women, black, white—generously giving their appreciation and kind words, validating the reasons we all were there. I felt an overwhelming sense of relief, almost of euphoria. This moment that had loomed enormously at the end of this long journey had come and passed. The fears, the anxiety of a million what-if scenarios that had not come to fruition, were past, and right then, surrounded by such acceptance, it was as though the weight of another person had been taken from me. It was more than I'd ever imagined and worth every second of trepidation I'd had.

As the crowd began to disperse and I gathered my things, a hand gently touched my arm. I turned to see a woman not much older than I, her face ghostly white, tense, as if she was doing everything in her power to keep composed. Leaning in close, she spoke almost in a whisper.

"My family was there that night, too," she struggled, her voice strained and halting. "I want to thank you for speaking for me."

CHAPTER 24

THAT EVENING AND INTO THE NEXT DAY, I rode a high like none other I'd ever felt. I couldn't really put my finger on the source of this emotion. Was it flattery, the knowledge that people appreciated and valued what I had to say? Was it the rush of simply being done with it all? Or was it deeper than that? There was certainly an element of forgiveness in the aftermath of the memorial. All throughout the day, I'd heard the words *forgiveness* and *atonement*. And I hadn't given either a great deal of thought, strangely enough. But maybe, deep down, I had a need to be forgiven. And if that was the case, my journey couldn't end that day. There was so much left I had to do.

The day after the march, I borrowed Catherine Ostos's PT Cruiser and drove through the pouring rain over the bridge into Superior, Wisconsin. Coasting along Highway 53, I watched for the turnoff to the town of Bennett, the site of the old Dondino homestead.

I hadn't really expected the town to be there; the postcards and photos I'd seen at home didn't show anything that I imagined would still be standing. Still, I hoped for a store, a service station, or maybe a school. The narrow road stretched in front of me, through fields, pastures, and groves with an occasional house about every mile or so, rustic houses probably over a hundred years old, and I thought there might be a chance that one had belonged to my great-great-grandparents. Mile after mile showed nothing but more of the same and with the exception of the Bennett Cemetery, where I would eventually locate my great-great-uncle Floyd and great-great-aunt Rosalie, there was no evidence that a town had ever existed. Undaunted, I pulled back onto the highway toward Solon Springs and the St. Pius X Catholic Cemetery, where I knew my great-great-grandparents William and Sarah had been laid to rest.

I rolled over the bridge, past a lone gas station and small bakery, coming to a stop at a corner restaurant. My MapQuest directions had gotten me this far; supposedly the cemetery was around here. I scanned the road signs for something familiar before looking up at the hill in front of me. Hidden behind the shrubs and outstretched branches of the low-lying trees was a clearing. A few bold headstones gave the place away.

The driveway into the cemetery wound up a steep hill and curved to the right. There was no one around, so I parked in the middle of the road at the top, stepping out into the lightly falling rain.

It didn't take long for me to find the family plots. A small wrought-iron fence separated the collection of Dondino and Dondineau markers from the others. The biggest one, a black, authoritative stone, rose from the ground as if holding court over the flat surface markers that surrounded it. William Dandenow, CO B.; 27 MICH. INF. Next to him, more recent and much smaller, was my great-great-grandmother Sarah's marker, a rectangular stone recessed into the ground. Except for a few faded, curled plastic flowers clustered between them, there was little indication that anyone had been there anytime recently.

I crouched down to read the inscription on Sarah's marker. 1845–1941. I breathed an unexpected sigh of relief as I calculated her age at her death: ninety-six. Each of my grandparents had died relatively young, the women between the ages of sixty-five and seventy-four, the men between seventy-eight and eighty-two, and so I'd always assumed that Shayne, who still had all four of his grandparents, would outlive me by decades. Here, at last, was evidence of the possibility of longevity in my family line. I had plenty of time left, even more than I'd imagined. I could do what should have been done eighty years earlier. An apology was one thing, but perhaps there was even more I could do. Even after a conclusion as glorious as the memorial, things still didn't feel completely right. Not yet.

I was sorry that my grandpa Ray had never returned to his roots, that he'd not come back to pay his respects to his grandparents after their deaths. I suppose his lack of religious faith made him feel there was no sense in visiting their burial places. He'd actually left for Mississippi two years before his grandmother Sarah's death. I thought of the time he spent with his grandparents as a boy and wondered how different it had been for him than it was for me. I'd spent summers with my grandparents both before and after my father was in prison. I like to think that my grandfather felt a kinship with me during those times, even if he wouldn't say it. Surprisingly, I think my life with my grandparents may not have been as different from his as one might think.

* * *

In 1971, Ray and Margaret moved from their home in Edmonds to a small piece of land in the forests off the Mountain Loop Highway, about sixty miles east of Everett. The highway runs from Lake Stevens up over Mount Pilchuck and around the other side to Darrington and back to Interstate 5. In spite of the fact that it is a loop, it's by no means a thoroughfare. Much of the road on the Darrington side is a narrow, winding gravel path that snakes its way downward for over twenty miles. The area to which they moved just outside the logging town of Granite Falls was, without a doubt, isolated. At the time, the few neighbors they had were seasonal, tiny mountain cabins that were inhabited only in the summer months.

My grandfather built their new house much like he'd constructed his family's lives. His means were limited. The tools at his disposal for creating and sustaining healthy relationships were not at all adequate; they consisted only of those experiences his difficult life had provided him. And so the framework of his family was shaky, at best. The same would be true for the physical construction of his and his wife's new house. He owned a simple collection of basic building tools, the variety that any weekend deck builder might have. His restrictive finances and satisfactory, but not superior, carpentry skills and expertise could supply only the most primitive living space.

Much of the material he used would be bartered for, purchased on the cheap, or even found. He cleared a small homesite in the center of the half acre of wooded land, using the stumps of the felled trees as a foundation for the slowly rising structure. Simple plywood subflooring and walls, single-paned windows, and rolled linoleum throughout, one bedroom, no bath. The home fit in well with the rustic weekend cabins scattered along the road that led past their home down to the river at the bottom of the hill.

Stepping into my grandparents' home was like traveling in time to a nineteenth-century homestead. The sea-foam green plywood wall with phone numbers scribbled on it next to the phone, the leaky roof and re-sulting percussion of water in aluminum pots and pans, the drafty win-dows, the floors that groaned under even a small child's weight—my memories of the place are truly heavenly. Except for the television (which barely picked up reception; sound buzzed and characters waved back and forth as if dealing with horrific spinal conditions) and the telephone (a party line shared with at least two other houses in the area) their house was one from much simpler times.

The home had been wired for electricity but had no plumbing, nei-ther indoor nor outdoor. Water for cooking or sponge baths was carried in buckets from a community spring near the river at the end of the com-mon drive. Some mornings I'd help my grandfather fill the white five-gallon buckets from the spring. He'd straddle the tiny creek bed, taking hold of the green rubber hose that seemed to grow magically from the ground, and I'd marvel at the simple ingenuity of it. "Hold that bucket steady," he'd say, "I don't want it dumping all over my feet."

The outhouse was one of the less glamorous elements of their rusti-cally charming home. Summer or winter, day or night, it was unbearable. If not the rankness and fly-bombarded swelter of a July afternoon, it would be the frigid, stick-your-rear-to-the-seat frostiness of an early Jan-uary morning. I avoided it altogether when I could, taking pride in the fact that I had a distinct advantage over my sisters when it came to tak-ing a leak in the woods.

The chilly days of winter were never a problem once you were inside the home; my grandfather made it his priority to keep a fire burning nearly twenty-four hours a day. Day and night, sun or storm, the stove raged. And the wood-burning cook stove where my grandmother spent a good deal of her day often augmented the fire from his potbellied stove, the crackling of cedar, the scent of embers mixed with oatmeal cookies filled the house with warm, delightful smells. She could cook, my grand-mother Margaret. Pot roasts, chicken and dumplings, biscuits, grits and the like came out perfectly, with only an old woman's hands to judge the temperature of the fire she'd stoked.

We begged our parents to take us to Grandma and Grandpa's house in the woods as often as possible, and the fact that the memories of those visits warms my soul even now, that my siblings and I still talk about them with such longing, illustrates just how special they were to us. And even though we saw my grandfather drink with a fair amount of vigor and regularity, and he could be an exhaustingly grouchy and cantankerous old man, we kids always regarded him as relatively harmless, a loveable (if somewhat abrasive) codger. He might grumble about a missing tool and accuse one of us of having moved it, or ramble on about how spoiled we were with our fancy cable TV and hot showers, but overall we laughed and ignored it as Grandpa just being Grandpa. We'd imitate him behind his back, hiking up our trousers, cupping our hands to our ears, and swearing in the privacy of the sheltered riverbed.

Coming home from the grocery store one day, my sister Karen and I sat in the bed of his pickup, crouched among the split cordwood and sacks of groceries, tumbling tail over teakettle as the truck swayed and sliced along the weaving mountain roads toward their home. The sides of the homemade canopy wobbled back and forth, a precarious structure not unlike a science project testing the bounds of physics. We pulled into the driveway and tumbled out over the tailgate, meeting my grandfather's curmudgeonly glare as he surveyed the overturned shopping bags.

"Goddamn it," he cursed, waving his arms at the mess. "You kids were playing around back here, getting into the food, weren't you?" We tried to show him the bumps, scrapes, and slivers caused by the hellish ride, but he was having none of it. It was our fault and nothing my grandma nor us kids said would change his mind. For the next two days, if there was an opportunity for him to bring it up, he did. Crusty old Grandpa.

My mother made sure our tetanus boosters were up to date before our stays in Granite Falls, as each of us had at one time or another had a nail from a discarded piece of lumber driven through the sole of our shoes. If we were feeling industrious, we might take a hammer and pound down a few dozen rusty spikes from the piles of mossy two-by-fours behind the house. Other times we'd gingerly scale the mound, evaluating the terrain along the way, wary of the tiny traps scattered throughout the yard.

*   *   *

My mother and Lenny had been together for just over a year when my sister Karen and I went for our two-week stay with our grandparents. She'd just turned sixteen, I'd had my twelfth birthday about two months earlier, and we both needed this visit more than ever. The legal process with my father had been going on for what seemed like months, with pretrial interviews, depositions, and hearings. I'm not sure that the actual trial had even started by then. The quiet reassurance of my grandparents' home was especially precious during this time; Karen could at last have some hope of putting our father out of her mind and I'd get a much-needed reprieve from Lenny.

Within an hour of jumping out of the car, Karen and I were climbing over the fallen cedar and into the thickets, reaching in and around the huckleberry brambles, plucking the small red berries from their twigs. A "ping" echoed from the bottom of the metal water pitcher with each one we dropped and we wrapped our conversation around our unfair lives, how we couldn't stand our mother's boyfriend, and how much happier we'd be living here in the mountains with our sweet, gentle grandparents.

The jug of heaping huckleberries rang on the silver Formica tabletop and two proud children beamed expectantly at their grandmother. "Oh, my!" she'd gushed. "I guess I'm gonna have to make a dessert tonight with these yummy berries!" She wrapped us in her full arms and kissed us. The slight aroma of freshly cut onions clung to her hands, mixed with the scent of Ivory soap. She pressed my face gently between her hands. "You two have been just as busy as beavers!"

Karen and I sank into the yellow vinyl chairs, the C-shaped legs springing easily under the weight of our bodies. I reached for the giant pickle jar that always held homemade cookies and slid it over to us. "Can we have a cookie, Grandma?" I asked.

"Just one," she said. "Don't wanna ruin supper." Spinning the lid, I opened the jar and fought with Karen for the biggest snickerdoodle.

"Where did Mom and Lenny go this weekend?" I feigned innocence, unconvincingly. "Do you know?"

My grandmother kept working at the counter, her back to us. "I don't reckon I do," she said quietly.

"Probably just staying in a motel or something," Karen said, a slight grin forming at the corners of her mouth. I hadn't thought of that, but then I wasn't the one who was sixteen and had spent the previous three weeks hitchhiking across the state with my best friend. "Probably just getting drunk."

"Karen!" scolded my grandmother, turning around. "Don't talk about your mamma like that!"

"Well they might be!" Karen laughed. "Lenny drinks a lot, you know." My grandmother shook her head and kept chopping away, silent but for a loud, exasperated sigh.

I pushed the chewed cookie to one side of my mouth. "Do you want them to get married?" I asked her, fishing for a reaction, maybe a little support for my side. There was a long pause and she put down the knife, wiped her hands on her apron.

"It ain't my business," she said lightly. "What your mamma does is up to her." She moved to the cupboard and grabbed a stack of plates, setting them down on the counter. None of them matched.

"But would you like it?" my sister pressed. "Do you like Lenny?"

"Oh now hush with that talk," she scolded, moving the stack to the table in front of us with a rattle. "Your mamma's a grown up and she can do what she likes; she don't need to ask nobody's permission."

"But . . ." I tried.

She ignored me. "Come here you!" she called into the living room and four dogs ranging from shin to knee high lumbered into the kitchen. She tossed a few scraps of bread on the floor and they dove for them like piranhas. The subject was closed.

That night, I organized the Lucky Lager bottle caps on the floor in front of me into rows. Those with word puzzles on the undersides took up the majority of the space; the blank ones would be throwaways once I'd completed the designs I wanted to make. The puzzles were keepers, though.

"Grandma?"

"Yes, dear." She rested in her recliner, crochet hook in hand, pulling and turning the shiny rod, churning out an ever-growing bolt of warmth.

"Are you going to come stay with us this Christmas?"

"If the good lord keeps me around that long, honey." I always hated that answer. It wasn't only the looming reality of her mortality that bothered me but the quiet, resolved acceptance with which she'd say it. That she was perfectly content with the prospect of leaving her family behind for an eternity beyond was sadly isolating to me.

"I'm sure you will be," I informed her, reassuring myself as well. And I was right. For three more Christmases, her heart would hold out to celebrate the birth of her Lord with the family. In August of 1982, though, she finally gave in to a body that had grown too weak for life and, as my mother had her grandfather, I would lose my beloved grandparent before I was old enough to drive myself to visit her. Unlike my mother, however, I knew it was coming and I had the gift of a goodbye, of holding her hand and knowing that it would likely be the last time we would tell one another "I love you."

The fire smoldered, a border of reclining dogs framing the black barrel-shaped stove with their pink bellies. My grandfather added a log, swung the door shut, and closed the damper. Karen lay on the sofa (my grandparents called it a davenport), and I had been tucked into the small cot pushed to the side of the wide hallway; he lumbered past me and into a small side storage room. When he emerged again, his arms were loaded with blankets—heavy, itchy wool throws that he proceeded to pile upon his grandchildren in layers. "This'll keep you warm," he promised, ignoring the sweat that was already soaking through our shirts.

My grandfather settled into the easy chair next to Karen, not far from me. The hiss of escaping carbon dioxide and the clink of a dropping cap, a sigh and a belch, elicited giggles from his grandchildren. Grandpa Ray was readying for his show.

"Let me tell you a story about a strange night," he began. "It was a night that the moon was blue and the grass grew upside down, with the roots sticking up to the sky. The cats chased the dogs and the birds swam." The story went on like that, no point and no direction, his voice humming into the night, his smile radiant even in pitch darkness. And I hugged my pillow, grinning and chuckling at the absurdities of a tale with no end until my mind finally drifted to sleep.

Back at the St. Pius X Catholic Cemetery, I shook my head at the absurdity of it all. What person would ever imagine a great-great-grandchild standing over his or her grave, let alone the outrageous event that had brought me there? I couldn't begin to think what old William and Sarah would have to say about this journey of mine, of my speech the day before. I have no way of knowing even what they felt toward their son after the crime or what their relationship with him was like after his release from prison. Perhaps Louis had come to Seattle after William's death. I know he left Minnesota prior to his mother's passing. Exact dates are sketchy, though the facts are clear: He never returned to the Great Lakes once he left.

"I don't know what you think of all of this," I suddenly found myself saying to the dark, weathered headstones. "But for what it's worth, you don't have to be ashamed anymore. Today, the Dondino name is something to be proud of."

* * *

Later that day, at a diner just down the hill from the cemetery, I nursed a cup of weak coffee between bites of an almost perfectly grilled ham and cheese. The diner was sparsely populated; it was well past lunch, after all. I looked around at the half-dozen or so faces as they laughed, whispered to one another, and sucked in drag after drag of smoke to thicken the blue haze in the room.

"Are there any Dondinos in here?" I wanted to ask. "Or Dondineaus? Dandenows? Dandeenoes?" There had to be some family left in this town, I imagined, and surely word would have reached a few that old Louis's great-grandson was coming to visit. No one had been at the memorial ceremony in Duluth, none that I know of. If they'd been there, they'd have likely stayed as far away from me as possible. I paid my check, left a generous tip, and headed back up the highway to Duluth, knowing that, like my great-grandfather, I'd never return.

THREE

WHAT MAKES A VICTIM? What moves a person from his identity as a human being to an object of hatred and violence? Throughout this journey, I'd asked myself the question over and over again, as it related not just to those at the lynching that infamous night, but to men and women today. What was it that led two young men to view Matthew Shepard first as a casual drinking companion, then as a thing to be pummeled and strung up to die? What compelled three white men in Jasper, Texas, to tie and drag James Byrd Jr. from the bumper of a pickup truck, traveling through the streets of their town until the man was so far beyond death that his body was no longer intact?

John F. Callahan, in his 2001 book, *In the African-American Grain: Call-And-Response in Twentieth-Century Black Fiction,* considers the nature of lynching violence as such: " Black slaves were not truly human beings or, if human, certainly not equal or endowed with any right to life or liberty beyond what their owners saw fit to grant." It makes sense, I suppose, the idea that one person must dehumanize another, completely objectify him in order to make the act of violence that much more palatable and justifiable. The origins—perceived superiority, fear, even religious extremism—seem unimportant. The end result, that overwhelming disconnect of one human from another, is the terrifying common denominator that I think each of us has the responsibility to keep at the forefront of our consciousness. It's like a short in our intellectual circuitry that gives us permission to hurt others.

*　　*　　*

Each time I looked at the postcard from the lynching, the grainy photo dark in image and in humanity, I wanted to know more. I could assuage my feelings by telling myself that my great-grandfather had simply been caught in the moment, but how could that rationalize such madness, remove responsibility from him and the thousands of others who were there? The faces looking back at me had seemed pure evil, certainly in light of what they'd been celebrating. And what of the victims? The young men, in their gruesome death poses, had been objectified in the coldest of manners, as cheap trophies displayed proudly on a gleaming mantelpiece. They had not been human to the mob that night, and the one-dimensional snapshot, trapping a singular instant, erases any shred of humanity from all who inhabit it.

"We tried to locate the families of the victims," Catherine Ostos had told me. "There just isn't enough information for us to use."

At the time of the lynching, the only information recorded had been the three men's names and assumed places of birth. Were it not for Elmer Jackson's bereaved father investigating his own son's murder, the young man's death certificate would still list his birth date as unknown and his place of birth, mistakenly, as Virginia.

In the days after the lynchings, six hundred and fifty miles to the south in Topeka, Kansas, a middle-aged shop worker picked up the June 16 edition of the *Topeka Daily Capitol*. "Three Negroes Lynched, Three Sent Back to Jail," screamed the headline. "Mob of 5,000 Successfully Overpowers Officers." This was shocking news for anyone to read given not only the dramatic nature of the event, but the location. If it had been in Mississippi or Alabama, maybe the impact would have been less. But Duluth? Up north? These things didn't happen up there.

It was something else in the story that had alarmed Clifton Jackson. "Circus workers," the paper said. One was identified as Elmer Jackson. His son hadn't used his Christian name in some time, preferring Ernest instead. Ernest had worked with the circus in years past, and it had been nearly seven months since Clifton had heard from him. To put his mind at ease, Mr. Jackson went to the Topeka courthouse, asking Deputy Marshal Charles Lytle to telegraph the chief of police in Duluth. Lytle did so, asking whether or not they had an Ernest Jackson listed as one of the victims. He was told no, "Ernest Jackson is not among the Negroes arrested or hanged here."

Not satisfied, Clifton went to Topeka Sheriff Hugh Larimer, requesting that he send a second telegram to St. Louis County Sheriff Frank

Magee. His reply was not at all reassuring: "One of the Negroes hanged here Tuesday was Elmer Jackson."

The coincidence was too remarkable; Clifton knew that he had no choice but to make the journey north, to identify the body. He contacted a local black attorney, Elisha Scott (who would later gain fame as one of the primary lawyers in the *Brown v. Board of Education* case), asking that Scott accompany him to Minnesota. If indeed his son had been murdered, and the details chronicled in the article were accurate, Clifton would not be finished with the city of Duluth on this one visit. Someone would need to pay.

Jackson and Scott arrived in Duluth on June 24, just over a week after the murders. It would be necessary to exhume Elmer's body, which had already been buried. The three men had been laid to rest in Park Hill Cemetery, a site owned by a local Lutheran church, a fact that had been kept somewhat secret; many Duluthians believed the men to be buried in a potter's field near the Duluth Cook Home (what was then referred to as the county poor farm).

Jackson and his companion ran into trouble practically the moment they arrived in the city. They had been told that the charge for an exhumation was five dollars, but the undertaker not only doubled the fee, he charged an additional three dollars for Scott as the witness. The men paid the money and the workers began digging. When the grave was opened, the sight that Clifton endured must have been absolutely excruciating.

Elmer had been buried not in a coffin, but in a crudely constructed box of slats. The dirt that covered his body and face had to be brushed away for better identification and when Elmer's face became fully visible, Mr. Jackson must have recoiled in utter horror. Elmer's face and body had been mutilated, his head crushed in as if "with an axe or hammer," as a local paper reported. Even so, it was painfully clear to Clifton that the boy before him was his son.

The widower Jackson struggled, like any man in his place would have done, to accept that after the tragic loss of his wife of over thirty years just twelve months earlier, he now had to cope with the death of one of his own children. He must have been relieved that at least his dear wife Rachel would never have to see what the bastards had done to her precious boy.

On the ride home, Clifton spoke intently with his attorney. They agreed that this was not over, not by a long shot. More than the few men who had been brought to trial shared the blame for what happened. The entire city bore responsibility and if they couldn't all be jailed, at least they would pay.

On July 3, attorney Elisha Scott filed suit on behalf of Clifton Jackson against the Duluth Police Department for failing to protect his son in custody, seeking $7,500 in damages. John E. Samuelson, a city attorney, minimized the claim, saying that city was not liable. In considering what likely lay ahead, Scott advised Mr. Jackson to drop the case and let his son rest in peace. Clifton did so, closing the book on the terrible event once and for all.

But Clifton's recording of his own and his late wife's names, as well as Elmer's place of birth in Missouri (and his hometown as Topeka), left a single dangling thread that would allow the possibility for someone, someday, to grasp hold and pull, to discover the human story of his son that had been ignored by the newspapers of his day. Amazingly, I had found it.

Each of us has a story worthy of telling, one that stamps our legacy and gives us the opportunity, in some way, to live on—even after we've passed. Elias Clayton, Isaac McGhie, and Elmer Jackson had the legacies of their own choosing stolen from them the night they were strung up and left to hang for the amusement of others. The images of their deaths have made an enormous contribution to the contemplation and exploration of human rights, social justice, and human understanding. They have become martyrs symbolic of the greater horrors of racism, dehumanizing hatred, and inequity that continue to this day. I felt surely they deserved a more personal remembrance than that.

The Clayton, Jackson, McGhie Memorial had gone a long way toward humanizing the men and portraying them as more than just "Negro circus workers." Artist Carla Stetson had made it clear from the outset what she wanted the sculptures to show.

"When the young men were lynched, they were depersonalized," she said in an interview during the monument's creation. "The idea of them being individual people with real feelings and their life in front of them—all of that was taken away. And so I felt like I had to reinvest these sculptures with personalities that were obviously individual people and really very realistic. Real people." Using models who had physical builds similar to the victims, she created expressive, beautiful faces for the figures.

In February of 2005, I gathered the stack of papers that I'd hoped would allow me to trace Elmer Jackson's life from his birth until the day he left for his final stint with the circus. I'd come to the realization that if I ever wanted to truly understand this man who was fatally connected to my ancestry, I would need to make a concerted effort to step as closely as possible in his footprints. Armed with a pile of nineteenth- and twentieth-century census data, a crudely sketched family tree, and a short article about a unique place called Pennytown, I left my home in Kingston, Washington, for the train yards of Topeka, Kansas, and the grassy hills of Saline County, Missouri.

CHAPTER 26

THOSE LAST MOMENTS OF LIFE for Elias Clayton, Isaac McGhie, and Elmer Jackson are forever seared into my brain. In the hundreds of pages of documents I've accrued, the witnesses' accounts and reporters' retellings of their deaths are, for me, the most precious. However upsetting it is to read, these are the only pieces of information in which they clearly speak to me; their words are their own and I can begin to feel an essence of who these men were.

For me, the most striking moment in the tragic narrative of that night is that of Elmer Jackson's demeanor—in his cell during the riot, at the base of the lamppost, just before his death. There is an odd complacency, an almost settled, quiet acceptance of the madness happening around him. According to one reporter, as the walls of his cell were being broken in, Elmer "stood beside his bunk, apparently watching with interest." While Isaac McGhie was understandably hysterical during his forced march to the lamppost, Elmer was noticeably silent. And then there was the moment in which he handed over his dice, stoically commenting that he'd had no more use for them.

I found the smallest clues to Elmer's character in those scenes, and reading them filled me with such great admiration for him and a longing to know more. What were the roots that nourished this man and helped create the strong person that he showed himself to be that night? Through further research, I began to learn about Elmer's life, about the Missouri slave culture that was the foundation of his family, and the atypical freedom that he'd experienced growing up in one of the few freed slave settlements in the area. I tried to construct a clearer picture of him, build a more complete structure of life around the framework that had been shown in those moments before his death. And I hoped to share it with his descendants when I spoke with them one day.

*   *   *

The world that had welcomed young Mack Jackson into its arms was not the nurturing mother of most newborns of the time. For a black child in 1845 Missouri, as in every other slave state, the laws and culture dictated that unless his parents were of the rare class of freedmen and freedwomen, he was owned the moment his lungs made their switch from fluid to air. When young Mack sucked in his first breath, the oxygen he took in was the only free element in his new life.

I was aware that there had been freedmen living and working in midnineteenth-century America, even in the South, but I hadn't known just how rare it was. Free "coloreds," as they were called, in 1840s Missouri comprised a very small amount, just 2.4 percent of the total black population: 1,478 freedmen to 57,891 slaves in 1844, to be exact. Saline County, where Elmer Jackson's grandfather Mack was born and owned, and all of the settled areas that hugged the rich, loamy soils along the Missouri River accounted for the majority of Missouri slaveholdings. A man by the name of Thomas A. Smith ran a moderate-sized farm in this region just over a hundred miles east of Kansas City. In 1844, he held title to seventy-seven slaves. This included families who, after emancipation, would settle together in a small hamlet nearby. Among those listed as Smith's slaves were Clifton, Mack, Louisa, Pleasant, Edmund, Nettie, and Aaron—all Jacksons who would pass their names down for generations to come.

Even before I began to learn of the Jacksons's roots, I'd assumed they had been slaves. I naively pictured scenes from films I'd seen, or books I'd read, Georgian mansions from a Faulkner novel, the fat, sweaty master swatting at flies, throaty cackling laughter as he surveyed his vast fields of thorn-riddled cotton bolls. But the great Virginia Tidewater and Kentucky Bluegrass slaveholders, with their expansive and dominating plantations that bring up images of Scarlett O'Hara dancing and sobbing under the cypresses of Tara, were a far cry from the smaller Missouri Boonslick slaveholders under whose thumb Mack was born.

With some exceptions, the number of slaves held by the typical Missouri upland master was as few as one or two, or in many cases, a single family. Very few families in the area owned more. I would learn in my readings that the majority of Missouri farmers were yeoman, affectionately referred to in many resources as "gentlemen farmers," who possessed small estates and worked their own land for their own families. I was surprised to find that it wouldn't have been unusual to see Saline County slaves working the fields of the area alongside the master and his sons. I imagine this would have made a marked difference in the self-image of the slave. It certainly wouldn't have taken the stigma of having been "owned" away, but I wonder if, in the slave's eyes, it didn't serve to tip the balance slightly between the roles of master and slave, watching your owner performing the same backbreaking work that you were. Would it have given that person a sense that, one day, he, too, could have acres of land, crops, and workers of his own? That he was just as much a human being as the white man working next to him?

This vision of a brighter future would also have been more visible for an upland slave, thanks in part to the greater family stability they were fortunate to have had. In the cotton-planted South, the antebellum slave trading often tore families apart leaving freed individuals with very little, if any, family linkage. Thankfully for Mack and his family, Missouri slave culture fostered a likelihood that the Jackson family and many others in the area might remain together, allowing generations of descendants to maintain a semblance of connection with one another. This isn't to say the lives of Missouri slaves were pleasant by any means—there were certainly whippings, lynchings, and plenty of viciousness to go around.

In July of 1859, four slaves were lynched in Saline County over a three-day period in incidents unrelated to one another. In one, an angry master chained his slave to a hemp brake, where he left him to freeze to death over the bitterly cold winter night, ostensibly "to teach him a lesson." In another equally grisly killing, a slave named John had been accused, using dubious circumstantial evidence, of the murder of his master's business partner. A screaming mob dragged John to a walnut tree that stood just a few hundred yards from the Marshall courthouse, where they gathered wood to his feet and set him afire. The local press decried the lynching, taking pains to point out the unexpected results of such carnage. "Many, very many of the spectators, who did not realize the full horrors of the scene until it was too late to change it, retired disgusted and sick at the sight," wrote a reporter from the *St. Louis Democrat*, adding, "May Marshall never witness such another spectacle."

*   *   *

As Elmer's grandfather Mack grew up, he'd have no doubt heard stories of lynchings like these and might have even come to accept them as an unpleasant part of life, much like the shoulder shrugs and matter-of-fact responses of "Well, that's just the way things were" that I've experienced repeatedly, as I've shared this story with others. While the constant possibility of violence would likely not have left his mind over the years, he and his family would have definitely been affected by the many changes happening around them.

Probate records for Thomas Smith, the master to Elmer's ancestors, show that his principle crops were corn, hay, and hemp—with his hemp holdings alone worth nearly as much as the other two combined. Prior to the Civil War, Missouri's principal cash crop was hemp, and harvesting this tough fibrous plant was backbreaking, exhausting work, so much so that no white person would touch it. Naturally, slave labor was crucial for hemp production to be profitable. A young male slave living on Smith's farm would have spent many hours in these fields with his father and brothers, while his mother and sisters performed domestic duties for the family such as cooking, washing, or general household work.

But with emancipation came enormous social and economic changes for Smith, his (now former) slaves, and the rest of southern and western America. For one, hemp farming found itself out of fashion and more or less defunct; importers began bringing in materials like jute as a replacement (lack of slave labor made the cost-effectiveness of hemp harvesting hardly worthwhile). The plantations were becoming decentralized and priorities had shifted toward the national marketing of crops and livestock. For Miami Township in Saline County, as in most all over Missouri, this meant that hemp was out; wheat was in. Between 1860 and 1870, the number of wheat farmers in the area tripled and wheat production increased almost tenfold.

I can't begin to imagine the world that greeted the Jacksons and their fellow freed slaves. Not only had the landscape of the farm fields in which they had toiled changed dramatically, their very identities had gone from one extreme to the other. One moment they'd been seen as nothing more than a piece of property, now they could proclaim themselves completely human, free, and whole. Being handed one's freedom had to have generated a great combination of elation, confusion, and crippling fear, especially for those whose entire lives had been lived in servitude to another. The only modern comparison might be to that of a career inmate turned back into society after a lifetime in prison. The task of reentering a world that wants nothing to do with him can be more terrifying than an eternity in bondage.

*   *   *

And so the Jackson family, as was the case with other freed slaves in the southern uplands, had not only to cope with the new frontier of personal freedom, but with the changing face of the farming industry in which they had developed their crafts. But their fortunes, and their destinies, would soon take a remarkable turn.

In 1850, thirty-five-year-old Joe Penny came to Saline County from Kentucky with his master, Jackson Bristol, with whom he remained until emancipation. Upon being freed, Penny moved to a small parcel of land just a few miles away from his former owner. Penny was a formidable figure, a man who made an immediate, strong impression on those he encountered. Stout, barrel-chested, he carried himself with a self-assuredness not commonly seen along the wagon ruts of Saline County roads.

He came to the area a childless single man, as far as the records show. Sometime prior to 1870, he married Harriet Butler, a freedwoman between one and six years his junior. (Census reports of 1870 and 1880 provide conflicting information. The ambiguity of census information for that time, especially in the cases of persons of color, was all too common.) Harriet had children of her own; in 1880 two of her adult daughters, Nora and Eveline Butler, lived in the home with Joe and Harriet. Also sharing the Penny home were two granddaughters and one grandson, Sallie and Minnie Butler and William Williams.

Until 1871, Joe had been a tenant farmer, renting and working a farm in the area. In March of that year, Penny and a white landowner named John Haggin completed a rare and unusual business transaction for the era: Haggin sold Penny eight acres of his land for the sum of $160, a deal that was duly recorded and filed with the recorder of deeds at the Saline County courthouse. This was possibly the only instance of the legal transfer of land to a freedman at this early period in history. Oral tradition holds that the white people of the area laughed at the sale of land to Penny, saying that it had only been sold it to him so that the law would know where to find him.

The details of the land purchase aren't particularly exciting, though it's interesting that the specifics of the sale vary by source. One written reflection indicates that Penny's purchase was forty acres and that, over the years, he parceled out plots "which varied in size from 100 feet square to five acres (to) members of his own race." However, other sources indicate that Penny sold the entire plot to his stepdaughter Eveline in 1873, continuing to live on the parcel with his family. Regardless of which story is accurate, the fact remains that Joe Penny, a freed slave, purchased a substantial amount of land that would later be owned and lived upon by dozens of families descended from slaves, in a former slave state. There would be an additional eleven transactions between white landowners in the township and enterprising blacks and, by 1879 there would be nearly sixty-four acres in communal ownership. The surnames of these families would forever define the hamlet that would be known first as Pennyville, then later as Pennytown.

In March of 1868, just before Joe Penny's monumental purchase, Mack Jackson married Christine Williams in what was then called the Colored Freewill Baptist Church. The wedding was officiated by Harrison Green, bishop; Mack was twenty-three years old, Christine twenty-one. Mack and Christine would have five children: Margret in 1868, Clifton in 1874, Tom in 1875, Edmond in 1877, and Mack Jr. in 1878. (A sixth child, an eight-year-old daughter, is recorded in the 1870 census, but the name is unreadable and no other indication comes up in future censuses so it's unknown what became of her.) Mack and Christine's family was one of several with the Jackson surname who settled in Pennytown.

Mack had always been a farmer and it was likely that his children would farm the land as well. In 1880, though, his chosen profession as listed in the census report had changed to "huckster," which involved gathering and selling whatever items one could collect and load on a cart: game, poultry, vegetables, eggs, tools, household items, and additional things that might be of value to others.

In my quest to understand the complex character of Elmer Jackson, seemingly fearless, certainly adventuresome, I realized that I must first seek to understand the uncommon settlement that was Pennytown, and the uniqueness of its founders and residents. The members of this collective enjoyed the powers and respect that property ownership brought, something that most freed slaves would never have the luxury of experiencing. This was unparalleled for the time and they had to have known it. They made the most of this opportunity, striving to create a settlement that provided for more than just their basic needs. They grew their own corn, tobacco, potatoes, and apples. They cultivated peach trees, raised chickens, produced molasses, hunted, and fished to provide for both themselves and their fellow Pennytowners. They had their own blacksmith and veterinarian.

Besides farming for themselves, Pennytown residents provided crucial labor for the neighboring farms and fields. They were reliable and, to a certain extent, valued outside of their village. To both its residents and the neighboring community of Marshall, the county seat, Pennytown stood in stark contrast to the black-settled section of Marshall labeled by both citizens and the official plat map as "Africa." While Pennytown symbolized opportunity and independence, Africa was the town ghetto, with all the stigma and lack of self-worth that came with the label. In the eyes of the white community, Africa residents were shiftless: they were loud and should best stay in their own part of town. Pennytown folks were hardworking and responsible—and, for the most part, content to remain in their own area of the county, far outside of town.

The white property owners surrounding Pennytown generally had a moderate level of respect for its inhabitants and would typically tolerate more from them than they would from the residents of Africa. A reflection by Bessie King, a lifelong resident of Marshall, shows a whimsical attitude toward her black neighbors.

"Oh, of course, an occasional chicken was lifted from a convenient roost, but at heart I think they were mostly honest and religious," she writes, adding that the residents were "really an asset to that part of the county.... Without Pennytown where would farmers have obtained laborers for their fields? Who would have helped the farm wives with many chores?"

The center of life in Pennytown was the Freewill Baptist Church. A structure that began as a simple wooden platform built under the shade of a tall hedge-apple tree, it sat just up the hill from a pond, one that served as both a watering hole for the livestock and a cleansing pool for baptisms. As part of such a close-knit community, the Jackson family would surely have been regular attendees at Sunday service. Worship, schooling, and family gatherings were held in this sacred spot; it's no wonder that the townspeople continued to give what little extra money they had to develop and sustain the church. Over time walls were raised, a roof built, and a real sense of permanence took hold.

It may be wishful thinking, but one wonders if the images of Elmer's quiet resolve on the way to his own lynching might have been rooted in this foundation of great faith. It's clear that deep spirituality played a role in the families' lives and in their perceptions of their own safety and well-being. It's interesting to read one person's reminiscence that, perhaps to ward off unhappy spirits or just as insurance to keep the good Lord in their midst, most Pennytown residents carried with them or memorized a piece of the Scripture, Ezekiel 16:6.

> And when I passed by thee, and saw thee weltering in thy blood,
> I said unto thee, Though thou art in thy blood, live; yea, I said unto
> thee, Though thou art in thy blood, live.

*   *   *

While no doctor ever actually lived in Pennytown, residents enjoyed a relationship of mutual respect and service with Dr. Tom Hall, a white man who lived just northeast of the hamlet. Dr. Hall allowed some flexibility for payment, accepting labor, meat, or produce instead of money if necessary. For the most part, though, families took care of their own medical needs. Shelves were stocked with all kinds of poultices for home remedies and medicines made from tree bark, weeds, and animals. Bags of asafetida, a pungent fennel-type plant, hung from children's necks to ward off germs. Skunk grease and quinine would be mixed and smeared on the backs and chests of patients with a cold or pneumonia. Skunk grease (skunks in Pennytown must have been a nervous lot) and goose grease were given for croup, and sugar, administered daily for nine days, was the suggested treatment for worms. Cherry bark figured into a good cough syrup, as did onion juice and sugar. Overall, the community kept a firm grasp on their health, with the exception of occasional bouts of scarlet fever (during which the residents installed quarantine signs on the roads and paths leading into the hamlet).

*   *   *

Sometime between 1891 and 1893, Mack's son Clifton (who was now between seventeen and nineteen years old) married a young neighbor woman, Rachel Smith, his same age. Soon after, Rachel bore their first son, Clifton Jr., and three years later on April 19, 1897, a second son was born: Elmer Jackson.

CHAPTER 27

Whenever a new child has come, a friendly neighbor is building a fire on

Wₕₑₙ I was very young, I asked my mother to tell me the story of when I was born, how big I was, whether or not I had hair—all the questions a child usually has of his or her first moments. She explained that mine was different than most births, that the doctors had to take me from her stomach because she just couldn't have me the way other mothers could. Then she'd show me the scar on her belly and explain that that was why my sister Karen had trouble learning, because the doctors didn't know they were supposed to cut my mother open when she'd given birth the first time and my sister had been injured trying to pass through the birth canal. I know the details of the day of my birth, the time of day, the hospital, the family members who would come to meet me. It's the beginning of my personal story, the first chapter of the ongoing book of my life.

I often wonder what Elmer Jackson's birth day would have been like, the details of his first chapter. Like the questions I asked my mother to create my first day, I searched for the cast of characters, the setting and the routines that created the scene for the day Elmer was born into this world. Taking what I've learned about the people of Pennytown, the births, the deaths, the moments in their lives, I like to imagine it like this.

The ground in front of Clifton Jackson's doorway is hard-packed, a delta of footprints fanning outward. The space under the lean-to porch of the simple one-room house is adorned with flag lilies and peonies, wild grapes and nuts, and maybe greens of wild mustard, tomato, and lamb's-quarter to welcome the new baby to Pennytown. As is the routine whenever a new child has come, a friendly neighbor is building a fire on the outdoor stone hearth and dunking the iron kettle into the rain barrel under the downspout to boil some sassafras-bark tea for Rachel Jackson, the new mother.

The morning glories winding themselves up and over the windows are just sprouting, so the day's light fills the room in a dappled display of warmth. Dr. Hall closes up his bag, satisfied that mother and child are stable and healthy as can be. Ducking past the lilacs on the way out, he bids farewell and makes his way home.

Elmer feeds himself the nourishment of love, life, and freedom as his mother cradles him warmly in her arms. Under the sage watch of a portrait of Abraham Lincoln, their emancipator, Rachel sings a soft, rolling spiritual and brushes the soft brown skin of her son's cheek.

It is a Monday, so most of the men in the neighborhood are working in the fields or at neighboring farms. The evening brings the sounds of singing as they return from a long day's work along the honeycomb of trails winding their way back into Pennytown. Neighbors Frank Payne, J. T. Lewis, Sam Lawrence, and Clifton's uncles Aaron and James and brothers Edward and Mack Jr. gather with Clifton at John Alexander's store to congratulate him on his new son, sharing words of wisdom over a plug of Horse Shoe or Granger Twist tobacco. Blue cigar smoke wafts on up through the oak branches, drifting over the roofs of the Price, the Barton, and the Moreland homes. It mingles gently with the gray billowing streams snaking upward from the King heaters that are warming the larger two-room homes of Dick Green and Ed Lewis (who, as legend had it, harbored the outlaw Jesse James on several occasions two decades earlier).

And perhaps Elmer's cry brings an amused nudge from one of the men, sending Clifton back to the house to check in on his new son. And on the way home, Clifton might dream for a moment of the life that his son has ahead of him, one filled with hard work, prayer, and opportunities that would not have been there for his father. Elmer will die an old man, his father says to himself, an old man rich in spirit, freedom, and in the love of his family.

CHAPTER 28

FOR EACH OF ITS RESIDENTS, it seemed that Penny-town provided a lifelong lesson in perseverance, dedication, and the cultivation of self-respect. Like every other child in town, Elmer would attend school at the Freewill Baptist Church under the instruction of a paid, trained teacher. A typical morning in the Jackson home would have seen dawn just breaking as the children began to stir from their beds. They'd have bid goodbye to their father Clifton as he left for the four- or five-mile walk to his employer's farm. If it was harvest time, he could typically count on double earnings for the day. Elmer's mother, Rachel, would be left the horse and wagon, which she could ride to her "family" for the domestic duties she performed for them. Sometimes they'd have paid her with money, other times her reward would likely have been scraps of meat, vegetables, or whatever else her employer could spare. If it was winter, hog-butchering time, Rachel would certainly have come home with wraps of hogs' feet, head, tails, chitterlings, and maybe enough liver for a meal.

While fresh water hadn't been a scarcity for them, it was definitely not a convenient commodity. Each morning before school, the children would have trudged the few hundred yards to the creek to fill their buckets for their daily sponge baths. Saturday nights in the Jackson home would have brought a special reward for a week's hard work: a hot bath. When Elmer was the youngest, he'd have been fortunate to have the washtub first, while it was still hot and clean. The rule dictated that the youngest in the family enjoyed the bathwater first, on up the line to the eldest.

Sunday church in Pennytown was more than just a time for worship — it was when the town gathered. In the summer, it was also the only time (other than going to town) that the kids of Pennytown covered their bare feet. Footwear was a luxury, handed down from child to child. If a child's shoes wore out when there was no money for another pair (as was often the case), Rachel, like most mothers in the village, would have done her best to extend their life, sewing tears and patching holes using a large darning needle and twine. A piece of sturdy paper or cardboard would have been cut to fit the soles to soften steps on the hard ground.

Sunday services were a time for spiritual validation and celebration of their savior and the bountiful gifts he provided them day after day. The joyous sounds of the gospel rang from the open doors across the hills of Pennytown, songs like "Deep River," "Get Right with God," and "Plenty Good Room in My Father's Kingdom." The sermon might be one of personal redemption or of humanity's penchant for violence.

Wars have always been a matter of concern, dread, misery and bloodshed from the beginning of tribes to the rising and falling of empires. Yet, like great volcanoes they are crushing, killing and leaving their sting of misery on millions. The human feeling toward peace seems to grow, yet steadily there lurks in the background that old spirit of an eye for an eye and a tooth for a tooth.

From "A Warless World" by Pennytown Freewill
Baptist Church Reverend James Jackson

In addition to the food they grew, Pennytowners relied heavily on the wild greens that grew in the fields and forests around them. In the spring especially, the children were routinely sent out to comb the grounds for wild lettuce, dandelion, thistle, carpenter's square, wild tomato, and poke greens. These would be cooked in the big iron pot over a blazing fire with a good-sized chunk of whatever meat had been brought home that evening. Poke greens were the poor-man's salad, and the white neighbors swore that the Pennytowners would poison themselves one day by eating the toxic plant. The trick was in the cooking, though, as the townspeople knew—cook them twice over, change the water between. Even local doctor Tom Hall defended them, telling his neighbors that the "greens won't hurt them if they put enough grease in them." What they didn't know was that Dr. Hall had been a regular guest for many a Pennytown supper.

Changing scenery, changing needs; even the peaceful existence of a tiny, communal haven could be a jail for those seeking more in life than what the hills and fields of Pennytown could offer. The world was waiting for Clifton Jackson and his family, calling to be conquered. So, sometime around 1913, the Jacksons moved from their little shack in Pennytown and made their way west, across the state line to Topeka, Kansas. Theirs had been the beginning of a gradual migration from the small settlement, though most Pennytown residents would move nearby, just to the edge of Marshall, settling in an area that would become known then as Stringtown.

At the time of the Jacksons' arrival, Topeka was a center of opportunity for the upwardly mobile, due in part to the Atchison, Topeka and Santa Fe Railroad, its major employer. The railroad yards acted as a crucial transportation hub for interstate railroad travel. With thirty-six stalls in its roundhouse, the train yard was world-class. In 1911, the building would become famous for constructing the largest steam locomotive in the world—the Mallet articulated locomotive. At its zenith, the shops employed over two thousand employees in a variety of specialties.

Those who had spent generations under the watchful eye of a field boss would have had much adjusting to do in this community of educated, literate citizens. Blacks in Kansas's capital city enjoyed an unprecedented level of political activity. Newspapers catering to the Negro community of 1916 Topeka show letters from readers ranging in subjects from race relations to current events. There were society pages recounting the activities and social goings-on of Topeka's more prominent black families; Mrs. Holmes Meade entertained informally at her home in Lincoln Street for Mrs. Frank Price on Monday, while Mrs. Jay Close was to entertain the members of her sewing club at her home in Polk Street on Wednesday. The autonomy and self-sufficiency that the Jacksons brought with them from Pennytown likely helped their transition to Topeka's progressive racial climate.

Black Topekans entering the twentieth century remained very active in local politics, arguing issues such as school segregation and interracial marriage. Kansans defeated a bill prohibiting such marriages in 1913 and rejected school segregation in Topeka twice, in 1913 and 1917 (although one would like to think this was motivated solely by social conscience, it appears that the primary reason was financial—too many schools, not enough students). The moves toward integration, however, affected only seventh- and eighth-grade students; elementary schools would remain segregated until 1954, when *Brown v. Board of Education* would nullify all segregation laws, putting Topeka on the civil-rights map. Blacks in Topeka were very aware of their current and growing civil rights, and the relative affluence of many of the residents kept local black lawyers busy. Membership in Topeka's NAACP was growing steadily and local black business leaders encouraged (practically demanded) cooperative business ventures and loyal patronage to black merchants and businesses.

In 1916, Clifton and his family lived at 1540 Kansas Avenue in the downtown area of Topeka. He had gained employment just up the street from his home as a porter in a building that housed Boer's Hat Shop, Milady's Frock and Beauty Shop, Underwood Typewriter, and the dental office of one W. B. Lockwood, among other establishments. Just blocks from the capitol dome, this was a good job for the son of a huckster, a man who had spent much of his life in the fields. Opportunities for success, especially when compared with the beautiful but sadly limited Pennytown, seemed endless.

Elmer, who by 1915 was nineteen years old, hadn't lived with his father during this time. His fascination for riding the rails and following the circus had led him to multiple stints doing just that. As there were several different companies operating at the time, he'd have had a variety of experiences working for them. Besides the John Robinson Show, early twentieth-century railroad towns could expect to see the Hagenback's circus, Ringling Brothers, Barnum and Bailey, and the Yankee Robinson Show, among others passing through. Elmer worked most likely as a roustabout, erecting and breaking down tents and other menial but laborious tasks. It was hard work, but Elmer wasn't afraid of breaking a sweat for fast, reliable cash. From the time the Jacksons moved from Pennytown up until early 1917, Elmer ran the rails several times—once staying gone for nearly three years while working for various carnivals and circuses.

In November of 1917, Elmer and his father Clifton began working in the Santa Fe shops, two of hundreds of mechanics employed by the railroad giant at the time. The long brick-and-glass buildings stretched the length of the surrounding tracks, smokestacks dominating the sky. The men spent hours a day amid the clamor of machines punching holes in boiler irons and pounding together engines while saws whirred in the carpentry shops. Many longtime shop workers suffered permanent hearing loss as a result of their exposure to the fierce and constant din.

In late 1919, Elmer had become restless and bored with the routine of his life. Perhaps the work in the machine shops became too monotonous for him, maybe the hours spent building train engines fueled his desire to see and hear them running, to be riding the open country again. His dear mother Rachel had died that year; Clifton struggled to care for his daughters Ruth and Rachel, ages nine and thirteen, and his seven-year-old son Reuben.

Elmer's sixteen-year-old brother Mack had fallen under the spell of the circus and left on his own that spring, much to his father's dismay. Elmer told his father that he was leaving Topeka; he wanted to visit family in Chicago. The truth was, Chicago would be a short stop, if he went there at all. The Chicago, Milwaukee and St. Paul line fanned out from the Windy City and would take him all the way up north to Minnesota; perhaps even westward over the Rocky Mountains through Montana to Washington State if he'd chosen. The open railway was calling and Elmer was ready to answer.

In January of 1920, Elmer Jackson found himself living and working at a small railroad camp in the town of Sioux City, Iowa. While the line through Sioux City had been completed over thirty years before, a great deal of repair and reconstruction was going on while Elmer was there. He shared the camp with over a dozen other workers, nearly all Greek immigrants. According to census data, Elmer was the only black man in the group.

The camp was located between the Big Sioux River and Military Road, in a part of town that is now known as Riverside. The river serves as a natural border between Iowa and South Dakota.

Elmer and the rest of the crew had landed a big job. Bud Smith is a Riverside resident whose grandfather was an engineer with the Milwaukee Road. He shared some of his grandfather's stories with Larry Obermeyer of the Siouxland Historical Railroad Association:

"(That) Sioux City camp rebuilt the railroad bridge that crosses the Big Sioux River just north of Military Road," Bud recalled. "The crew had to pour new footings and pilings, as well as reconstruct the bridge roadbed and framework to accommodate larger locomotives and heavier trains."

"Bud didn't know how long the camp was in Sioux City," Larry told me. "When they completed their work here, they moved north along the line to set up additional camps to build bridges where the railroad crossed the Big Sioux."

The location of the Military Road camp was closer to the grocery store and local bars than to the work site, the better to accommodate the "interests of the workers," Obermeyer quipped. While local children would often catch bullfrogs to sell to the black men who worked at the roundhouse, they generally stayed away from the camps. Besides drinking, gambling was a common activity enjoyed at the camps, dice being a particular favorite. And any mother would have warned her child that liquor and dice alone are bad enough; the combination of the two was a sure-fire recipe for trouble.

A cast-iron backbone and a solid level of confidence would have proven invaluable to Elmer at this time. It would have taken brains, smooth talking, and guts for a black man in 1920 not only to set off alone on the rails, but place himself in the middle of a crap game with fifteen white men, immigrant or not, northern state or southern.

Some time prior to April, Elmer returned to the rails and made his way east, perhaps back to Chicago, but more than likely he took the Chicago line through the city south to near the end of the line. The John Robinson Circus had its home base in Peru, Indiana, and if Elmer spent three years working the circuses in his youth, he would have been well aware of the small town in central Illinois that (due to the several circus companies based there) billed itself as Circus Capital of the World. On April 24, 1920, the Robinson show departed for what was to be one of its largest tours, playing 159 days and covering over 16,000 miles. It was to be the ninety-seventh annual tour for the circus, and the final weeks of young Elmer Jackson's life.

CHAPTER 29

T<small>HE HIGHWAY LEADING OUT OF KANSAS CITY</small>
quickly became a desolate and lonely stretch of landscape, headlights
panning over roadway that seemed to have no end. I'd not experienced
the topography of the Midwest before that visit in February of 2005, and
for a man born and raised in the Pacific Northwest, sandwiched between
the Olympic and Cascade mountain ranges with volcanic peaks to the
north and south, the flatness of the expanse was stunning to me. Early
winter, before the snows come, is the perfect time of year to truly appreciate the laconic mood of a drive through the Kansas countryside. In the
dead of night, with only the slightest of moon glow illuminating the
whispering fields, it's like a drive over an endless bridge that stretches
across a vast ocean. A lone naked tree reaches upward here and there, intermittent explosions in an otherwise uninterrupted plain.

My lights panned across a billboard for the Oz Museum in Wamego,
Kansas. For a second I was sucked in, imagining a farmhouse somewhere
that Judy Garland and her cohorts had used while filming. Thinking of
old Hollywood soundstages and backdrops, I laughed at my naiveté and
continued frantically hitting the scan button on the radio, listening intently for the familiar soothing, clear voice of National Public Radio.

I pulled into the parking lot of the hotel at last, the place that would
be my home base for the next five days—a too-short whirlwind of a visit.
Conveniently located next to the freeway, the hotel had once been a Hol-
iday Inn in what had likely been better days for both the city of Topeka
and for the hotel itself. It was currently undergoing a slow, major reno-
vation by its current owner, who was generously allowing me to stay in
his building free of charge. This had been coordinated by my new acquaintance and local contact, a civil-rights activist named Sonny Scroggins, with whom I'd been communicating via e-mail.

I'd connected with Sonny when I'd learned of the Elmer Jackson
Memorial Bridge in Topeka, a project undertaken by Scroggins and his

organization, Bias Busters. Sonny had learned of the Duluth lynchings in 1991, when a group of citizens in Duluth had held a small ceremony to dedicate plaques for the previously unmarked graves of Elmer Jackson, Elias Clayton, and Isaac McGhie. He'd been invited to contribute his words, as a representative of Elmer's hometown. Inspired by the group's actions, he'd convinced the Topeka city council to rename a bridge near the former Jackson family home in Elmer's honor. Sonny was glad to hear of my continuing work in uncovering Elmer's story and had graciously arranged for my stay in Topeka. When he asked if I would speak on a local morning radio show and participate in a symposium on Black History Month, I immediately agreed.

It was after midnight when I checked in; the desk clerk was polite but sleepy in spite of the atomic glare from the impossibly shiny lobby floor. The entrance was vintage 1970, but meticulously clean and orderly. I rode the elevator to the top floor and stepped out into the dull glow of the long hallway. The numbers on the doors were intermittent—some polished brass, others on paper index cards taped above the glass peepholes. I was exhausted and pleased to find that, other than the chilly breeze that continued to spill from the vents (no matter what I did with the thermostat), the room was clean, comfortable, and welcoming.

At eight the next morning, the phone rang. Rubbing my eyes, I clumsily picked up the receiver.

"Hello?" I croaked.

"Mr. Read." It was Sonny and he wasn't asking if it was me, he was telling. "Welcome to Topeka."

"Thank you," I said. "It's good to finally be here."

"I'm going to give you a name," he informed me. I scrambled for a pen, without questioning him. Just as I suspected from his brief, direct e-mails, Sonny was a commanding presence, even over the telephone. A man of few words, he spoke to me as if I should know who he was and what he was about to say. In the movie *Pulp Fiction*, Ving Rhames plays Marsellus, a fiercely intimidating crime boss who scatters people with one look. Sonny was Marsellus, informing me that this person would be calling and that I should be ready. He left the rest of the details unknown, bidding me goodbye until later. I sat up in bed, terrified that I might miss the next clue to the mission.

165

An hour passed and, with a laundry list of things to do—the Kansas State Historical Society library, the Topeka public library, the Jackson home sites, the memorial bridge—I couldn't wait any longer for the phone to ring. Hesitatingly, I gathered my things and left. (The call never came. To this day, I don't know what important message I missed, but there was no apparent fallout that I could see.).

The hall outside my room was as bleak in the daytime as it was when I arrived the previous night. I made my way to the elevator, pushed the button, and waited. And waited. And waited.

"Elevators must be busy," I thought. "I'll take the stairs."

I left the eighth-floor corridor behind, making my way down the cavernous stairwell toward the lobby at the bottom. Finally, I reached what seemed to be the ground floor, a dead-end blocked by a door covered in loud red lettering. Emergency Exit Only, it warned. Alarm Will Sound! I retreated, thinking I'd just overshot the correct floor. One flight up, I opened the door and went back into the building.

The corridor stretched endlessly in front of me, dark and abandoned, the carpet an unsettling pattern of splatter stains and wear. Light shone through empty knob holes in several doors, giving polka dots of guidance as I made my way down the hallway in search of a way out. With the only doors open leading to empty, gutted rooms, there was no apparent exit other than the unresponsive elevator and the stairwell that led back to the forbidden door.

I returned to the stairway, stopping at nearly every floor on my way back up, each diversion another walk through the haunted hotel that lay beneath my room. Even when I reached a floor in which many of the rooms seemed operational, the ghostly aura that enveloped the hallways was like a Midwest version of *The Shining* and I half-expected to see a former resident's spirit come sailing down the hall toward me.

A half hour later, I emerged from the building thanks to a chance encounter with a cleaning cart and a friendly maid back on the eighth floor. Mopping my forehead and flipping my shirttails up and down in an effort to cool my borderline anxiety attack, I drove out of the parking lot with a rudimentary map of Topeka.

My first destination was the most recent Jackson home at 1403 Quincy

Street, where Clifton and his family had lived in 1920. Within a mile of the hotel, the Fourteenth Street sign sprang into view and I quickly pulled to the curb.

Walking up and down the block, disappointment took hold of me as I realized that the house numbers ended at 1405: a vacant lot languished where the Jackson house had once stood. An imagined vision of the structure could still be had, though, as every other house on the block still stands as built. The familiar pitched roofs and covered porches that were universal in working-class suburbia after World War One line the street like a faded postcard of early Americana.

As if it had been cut neatly with a giant cleaver, the sidewalk ends at the empty parcel of land. A row of tall oaks lines the length of the block, reaching over the walkway that stretches in front of the homes. Curiously, there are no oak trees beyond this point, either. The corner has the blunt appearance of having been wiped completely clean, with nothing but close-cropped, brown lawn in place of what had once been there.

Climbing back into my car, I drove toward the second stop of my morning, the Elmer Jackson Memorial Bridge. Along the way, I passed the old Monroe Elementary School at Fifteenth and SE Monroe, now the Brown v. Board of Education National Historic Site. It's a beautifully re-stored brick-and-mortar building that stands out curiously in a neighborhood of homes that seem to be trying to do everything they can to blend in with one another.

Sonny had given me general directions to the bridge near Fifteenth and Adams and I nearly drove across it before I noticed the tiny green marker. An imposing white traffic sign blocks the marker from view when approaching from the west. Pulling alongside the road I walked up the slight incline, over the railroad crossing and up to the concrete road-way that spans the sluggish Shunganunga Creek.

I hadn't imagined that the bridge would be anything visually special. I hadn't expected a quaint covered bridge from a lovely storybook romance. Still, even with my low expectations, I was underwhelmed. This bridge was tucked so far out of the way, so ignored, that I wondered who, if anyone, would even take notice of its significance. The marker displaying Elmer's name was overshadowed even by the loud yellow diamond mounted above it, warning drivers to watch for ice on the bridge.

The ceremony in 1992 naming the bridge in Elmer's honor had been equally subdued. Craig Grau, associate professor of political science at the University of Minnesota, who had spearheaded the effort to provide monuments for the lynching victims' graves, had attended the dedication of the bridge with Sonny and three activists from the local NAACP. "The bridge was defaced the night before, and there was a tense feeling that day," he recalls.

Church elder Carl Bryant had given the invocation, and he had exhorted listeners to trust in Christ and assuage their pain by following in his steps. Elder Bryant's wife had remained in the car; her health was poor. When Grau spoke with her, she shared her vivid memories of having played with the Jackson children in her youth. She remembered Elmer's younger siblings well and recalled that the family left Topeka for California some time after the lynchings, though she couldn't specify when.

As I trudged through the tall grass above the banks of the dark water, I lamented the lack of prominence given to Elmer's name on this site. Cars drove over the bridge at the rate of about one a minute. How many even noticed the sign? Ever? I'd hoped to be able to ask a passerby or neighboring business owners what they knew about the man whose name was under the ice warning, but there was nothing and no one around. A fence company, its stark chain link looming and uninviting, was the sole building in sight. Then, I felt a jolt of optimism and indulged in a bit of wishful thinking.

Maybe the seclusion of the bridge and its marker would be a question mark—one that would scream for an answer from some driver or a curious student one day. "Who is this Elmer Jackson and why is this bridge named after him?" An inquiry would be voiced, a search done and a new discovery would be made. Elmer's story. This bridge, however unexciting and drab, would insure that this Topeka resident, unlike many of us, would never be completely forgotten.

From the bridge, I drove to Clifton's former home, the address he'd listed when he worked as a porter after arriving from Pennytown. Like their later home at Quincy Street, 1540 Kansas Avenue was the sole vacant lot on the block. Kansas Avenue is now a busy thoroughfare, clotted with convenience stores, taverns, and, like Quincy Street, small used-car lots.

I sat in the car, frustrated and lost, feeling like I'd been dropped in place by a badly calibrated time machine. The naked squares on which the Jackson's houses had once stood, even the ghostly hallways of the hotel, were but neglected remnants of an earlier era, frozen in time as they waited for the next visionary or charitable donor to modernize them, to make them habitable again. Or, perhaps they simply waited to be subtracted from the total, erased completely from the earth as if they had never existed.

*　　*　　*

In 1986, I made a special trip to Granite Falls, just me and my ten-year-old Ford Pinto, sputtering our way up the highway to the tiny mountain shack that had been my grandparents' home. My mother had just sold the acre under it—there had been no value in the empty, abandoned house. I knew that the house would be leveled at any moment; it might even have already been destroyed for all I knew. But I had to see it, to walk through the gate one last time.

It had been at least a year since my since my widowed grandfather's stroke had gifted him with a quick delivery from his loneliness and I'd expected that when I pulled into their driveway I would find a neatly flattened grid of dirt where the house had been. My mother had learned when trying to sell the property after her father's death that it didn't matter that her parents could never afford a septic system; the drainage on the property was so terrible, they'd have been unable to install a septic tank anyway. Because of this, the lot was nearly worthless. So it was sold to a neighbor for a fair price. We understood that it would likely become a natural extension to his own lot, an open space of sod and young saplings. As I rounded the bend, I was shocked to find the house still standing upright—more or less. Not thinking about trespassing, I stepped through the gate that now hung tiredly from its hinges and made my way up the overgrown driveway to the front porch.

The sagging boards of the mudroom groaned under my shoes as I walked through the open doorway. The familiar blue linoleum flooring peeked up from beneath the newspapers and trash that lay scattered around the room. The house had long since been picked clean of any items of value, monetary or otherwise; the structure remained as is, waiting for the bulldozer that would eventually come to push it all away, gone forever. I moved to the kitchen, stepping down into the massive concave indentation; the rotting wood beneath gave way as if some giant fist had smashed it that much closer to its unavoidable demise. I turned to leave, and something caught my eye.

A small plastic bag lay crumpled in the corner of the room, a flash of red peeking through. A pair of hot pads, a simple crocheted design— nothing special to the person who would have made a final pass through here before pushing in the walls. I'm not sure what my grandmother had thought of them. It probably had been a quick project that she'd bagged for a possible gift later, thinking there would be a later. And the wonderful thing is that it came to be in that moment; there was a later, and the gift was for me. I opened the bag and held the wool squares to my nose and breathed in. And for a brief moment, the house was toasty warm, the biscuits were cooling on the counter, and my grandmother was next to me broadly smiling, a dollop of flour lightly powdering her cheek.

I left my grandparents' house holding desperately on to that vision, the memory of a moment that brought a tearful smile. I know today that there is nothing on that site that would remotely suggest that Ray and Margaret Dondino had ever existed or that I had spent countless afternoons searching for caterpillars behind the Douglas fir-covered nurse log, or that the torn hearts of young children had been carefully mended by the gentle hands of a sweet old woman in the summers and an occasional weekend.

*   *   *

Traveling through Topeka, I couldn't help but feel a similarly wistful longing, a desire to see clearly a picture of happier days. Here was a community clearly struggling in uneasy economic times, its very framework sagging under the weight of the inevitable passage of time. Outside the downtown core, like many towns in which the growing sprawl creeps outward, the landscape is pockmarked with strip malls, ninety-nine-cent stores, and sadly weathered homes that at one time must have commanded great admiration and pride. Entire blocks of grand colonial and Victorian homes, paint peeling, yards muddied, spider-web window cracks covered over with silver duct tape, stand as ghosts of an era gone by. Each neighborhood I drove through, every house I passed elicited a feeble aura of what it might have been decades before; my mind invented memories for my surroundings that were nothing more than wishful thinking. What I wanted for Topeka was really what I wanted for myself: proof that the Jacksons had been here, that they mattered, that they were, in fact, still living among the ghosts of Topeka.

CHAPTER 30

THE RAILROAD SHOPS OF TOPEKA still command a centric presence. Smokestacks rise from the yards in seemingly random fashion, their towering forms visible from a fair distance—generous guides for the directionally challenged driver trying to make sense of a poorly printed map. On the edge of town, the pale sand and deep-red-brick buildings stretch along the tracks, occasional perpendiculars breaking up the monotonous pattern. Ironically, the simple rectangular design of the shops with uniform rows of tiny windows lining the sides elicit the image of giant abandoned railcars, their former passengers having moved on to a more welcoming place long ago.

The neighborhoods immediately surrounding the shops are probably the poorest and most rundown in the area. Tiny bungalows sit on matchbox-sized lots, porches overflowing with garbage and clutter, front gates open to cracked, weedy walkways leading to darkened front doors. Up and down these blocks, former shop-workers' homes limp into the new century as sad remnants of a booming era whose time has passed.

*　*　*

The car was parked facing the train shops but my eyes focused instead on the rearview mirror, glued to the scene playing itself out behind me. I saw a filthy white house ringed by short slat-woven chain link, with a crippled sedan propped on blocks in front. There was a flurry of activity as a man slid from under the car. He sat up, his head tilting back as he called out something, and within seconds, a young boy, about eight years old, jeans too short for his gangly legs, came running around the back of the car. The two exchanged a few words and the boy turned around, darting away as the man laid back down on the tarp and returned to his place under the car.

Less than a minute ticked by and the boy returned, carrying a fistful of shiny silver wrenches. He handed them under the car and then a strange thing happened, something that to me seemed utterly incomprehensible. The boy stayed. He scooted close to the edge of the car and leaned down to get a better look.

*   *   *

My memories of working with Lenny on the car, playing gofer for his tools, had been lessons in random searching, mind reading, and second-guessing myself. He'd ask for a nine-sixteenths open-ended wrench and I'd frantically begin digging through the clutter of his toolbox, racing against his quickly fading patience. My heart would pound, my mind jumbling the fractions, and before long he'd drag himself from under the car and lunge at me, pushing me out of the way. He'd curse, accuse me of lacking the tiniest amount of brain matter, and I'd spend the rest of the day wishing I could be anywhere but within arm's reach of him.

*   *   *

I started the engine, keeping my eyes on the vibrating reflection in the mirror as I pulled from the curb, the warmth of the heater enveloping my feet like a blanket. If I had stayed close to the toolbox, if I had been as eager to help as that little boy, I wondered whether Lenny and I would have been able to forge some kind of bond based upon car parts and hard labor. I had fought any attempts to align my own interests with his, and once I realized I could never meet his expectations, I stopped even trying. Perhaps there had been a chance after all to make it work. Then again, maybe it had been unworkable and I'd done the best thing possible by keeping my guard up all those years, holding off any kind of a relationship with him.

I returned to my chilly hotel room spent with a splitting headache, my stomach crying out for food. On the way through the lobby I asked the front-desk clerk to recommend a restaurant and she unenthusiastically pointed out an Indian diner up the road a few blocks.

I left the hotel with an eerie sense of isolation, a feeling of displacement as I contemplated the fact that, in spite of having been given my room free of charge, having agreed to be a keynote speaker at an event that was to happen in the hotel conference room in two days, there had been no acknowledgement of my presence whatsoever (with the exception of Sonny's cryptic phone greeting that morning) by the hotel staff or management. I'd been developing a strange loneliness since I'd arrived and with it a growing level of guilt for expecting anything more than complete anonymity. Of course, had anyone tried to impose on my time I'd have been irritated for the intrusion on my privacy, so I suppose there would be no pleasing me at that moment.

As I crossed the near-empty parking lot, I looked up the hill toward the restaurant. I could see the white signage jutting out from the side of the building and my hunger pangs intensified. But something more interesting was happening just across the street from it, further up the sidewalk. There seemed to be a small group of people clustered together and I could hear shouting—not an angry exchange at all, more like a frantic message or plea of some kind being called out above the crowd. I wondered what kind of excitement I might have been missing as I'd been sitting in my hotel room and thought I might put off dinner for a few more minutes so I might see what all the fuss was about.

As I got closer to the crowd, I saw about a dozen people, adults and children, carrying picket signs, while theatergoers made their way to the performing arts center on the corner. Individuals and families walked around the picketers, ducking under signs and into the theater, seeming to pay the demonstrators no mind whatsoever. It was as if this had been a years-long strike in which everyone but the participants had long ago stopped caring. When I got closer I realized that this was no labor union dispute. I recognized the multicolored placard immediately, as well as its message: God Hates Fags. It was the infamous reverend Fred Phelps, hatred-spewing minister, and his family of fellow homophobes marching up and down the block. Even the smallest of children walked in step with their parents, blindly waving messages of vitriol they likely couldn't even read.

I forced a smile, if only to deflect the smears and daggers designed to cut me. I had long ago become familiar with Fred Phelps and the crazy Westboro Baptist Church family. Even in Topeka, an easy notch in the Bible belt, the group exists in isolation, both in their own eyes—they see themselves as stand-alones in the sinful world of hedonists—and in their extreme interpretation of the Bible. They're the group that picketed Matthew Shepard's funeral in Laramie, Wyoming, announcing that he would burn in hell for his sins; they're the group who likes to demonstrate at the funerals of fallen soldiers, blaming their deaths on "America's tolerance of fags."

Even today I am puzzled by this group's obsession with sexuality and their undying need to demonize gay people or anyone associated by the most slender of threads to homosexuality. Even Lenny, a man who did nearly everything in his power to make me hate both him and myself, never gave me reason to think that a person's sexuality was fodder for ridicule. His sister-in-law was a lesbian, and although he made plenty of cracks about her weight, he never disparaged her lifestyle. I learned later that he had had an aunt who was born a hermaphrodite, who ultimately killed herself rather than live in a world in which she had no place.

The last time I saw Lenny was on a Friday night in October of my senior year of college, my first weekend home to visit my mother. She and Lenny had been apart then for several years. Finally free of the codependency of their marriage, she and I had begun to repair the strained relationship we had had over the last decade. It had been a time of much "personal work," as she describes it today, a time to gain a better understanding of the complexities of growing up with an alcoholic parent and, ironically (as often happens), having married an alcoholic as well. It had been the beginning of a long path of reconciliation for us, of making amends for unhealthy decisions and clouded judgment.

On this particular visit, I'd been feeling particularly needy and she'd been unavailable to me, on the phone for over an hour, gossiping with a friend. I left, storming out of the house in a cloud of self-righteousness and disgust. Across the street was the Buzz Inn, a restaurant and lounge of the same genre as the Townhouse and the Kozy, though a few notches above. I knew I could stew there for awhile and allow my mother to feel guilty until I came home.

I pulled on the cold metal of the door handle, rattling the sleigh bells wired to the door, and stepped into the haze of cigarette smoke. An odd couple caught my attention; a plain-looking woman not much older than I was, dirty blond hair hanging over her eyes, sat next to a man old enough to be her father. He was hunched over his ashtray, his cheeks hollow as he sucked a power drag from his cigarette, his eyes closed like he was concentrating on every milligram of nicotine that was filling his lungs. It was Lenny. He opened his eyes and looked over at me, giving me a look of surprise and uncomfortable recognition.

I steeled myself for a confrontation. Remnants of our most recent interaction hung stagnantly in the air and for a moment I thought about turning and leaving. The weekend after high-school graduation, I'd moved out of the house. He'd come by to visit and, apparently, inspect my room. It wasn't clean. He yelled at me, I yelled at him. He left in a huff and that had been the last time I'd seen him until now, four years later.

He stood up and waved me over to sit in the booth with him. I thought it was important to be cool, to be an adult and go along with it, so I sauntered over and took my spot across from him and the woman I would learn was his girlfriend.

"So," he said, smiling as I sat down, "what have you been up to lately?" It was a genuine question this time, I thought, not one designed to confuse or trap me or make him look superior at my expense.

"Just school," I told him. "I'm in my last year."

"Yeah, I heard," he said. He pushed a basket of fries toward me. "It sounds like you're real busy." He wanted to know what had brought me into the restaurant and I told him I'd been mad at Mom, that she'd been on the phone ever since I'd walked in. He laughed and told me that if she was talking with Eleanor, I could relax for at least another hour. "Here," he said, "I'll buy you a Coke."

"So," he asked, "you got a girlfriend?"

I shifted uncomfortably in my seat. "No," I said. I thought about giving a reason, but he interrupted.

"A boyfriend?" This time he waited, allowing me the opportunity to give whatever I wanted.

"No," I said again with a defensive laugh as I shook off the very notion. I twisted my face to show just how off-base he was, my cheeks flushing in obvious contradiction. He laughed in return. "Whatever," he said. "It's cool."

And then we talked; like two grown men, we conducted a full-on conversation and anyone who didn't know the sour aura hanging over the two of us would have thought we were just a couple of old buddies shooting the breeze. He told me about his work, about the big pipe-laying job he'd been on in Issaquah, and gave me an update on all the familiar names of his buddies in the company. And when I talked about my job, my classes, he listened and told me it sounded like a pretty good deal up there in Bellingham. He said he could tell that I'd lost weight, and that I seemed in good spirits.

"You look real good," he said. "I can see you're doing real good for yourself."

My chest swelled and for a second I thought I might reach across the table to shake his hand or pat his shoulder, but I just nodded and said, "Thanks."

As I finished my Coke, he asked if I was hungry for a burger and told him no, that I was planning to eat with Mom, as long as she still had energy after her marathon phone call. I got up and he did the same. We stood opposite each other like gunfighters, our arms nervously at our sides, neither one of us knowing what gesture was appropriate as we completed our first agreeable conversation in memory.

"It's good to see you," he said, smiling and nodding his head slowly. "You too," I said, nodding in response. As I walked toward the door, he called out for me to say hi to my mother and to keep out of trouble. I said that I would.

*　　*　　*

I stood at the chilly corner in downtown Topeka, my hands buried in my coat pockets, and watched theatergoers weave through the picket signs. I wondered if it wasn't actually a good thing for Topekans to have such an exaggerated caricature of intolerance in their community. Would a father, walking with his son past a particularly nasty sign, comment on how ridiculous and unfair it was? And would that small seed of tolerance grow and actually flourish within that child to one day create an informed, accepting young man? I like to think so. I love the idea of that very thing coming from those god-awful signs.

I retreated from the crowd, and walked back down the hill, leaving the Phelps family behind me to wallow in their own stink. How tragic, I thought, to spend what little time one has on this earth funneling one's energy and selfish fears into hatred and intolerance. And I thought about the isolation that Elmer must have felt his last night on Earth, the sound and the fury of the mob seeking to kill him both for who he was and what they thought he'd done. The same had been done to Matthew Shepard in Laramie, and if Fred Phelps and his family had their way, they would do the same to me.

CHAPTER 31

INTERSTATE 70 WINDS THROUGH Kansas and Missouri, slicing neatly through Kansas City (both of them). It passes through alternating scenery of expansive wheat fields, truck stops, farms and silos, and an occasional oddity I'd not seen in my relatively liberal home state of Washington.

I know that this great country of ours is home to a complex myriad of needs, values, and lifestyles. I knew that the Midwest would be a different landscape than my own hometown, both geographically and politically. Knowing that I would be traveling to a relatively conservative region, I was therefore both confused and amused by an unexpected feature of the Kansas-Missouri roadway.

Buxom blondes, glistening lips whispering an invitation for "HOT,

SEXY DEALS" and "XXX FUN, NEXT EXIT" popped up like an advent calendar of titillation. Nearly every off-ramp that led to a gas station or truck stop skirted a porn shop, flashing lights and flapping flags drawing in the lonely, weary traveler looking for a pick-me-up on his way home from a long haul or maybe just the grocery store. So I found it ironic that this region, which is perceived to have its eyes firmly directed at morals and strength of character, would take such a unique approach to perking up its weary, lonely drivers. We have Starbucks for that kind of thing.

Pulling off the interstate, I drove past the Fireworks Outlet and its neighboring adult store, north up Highway 65, past Blue Lick, Missouri, to Marshall, the Saline County seat. I was scheduled to meet with the town historian at the library; I was running ahead of schedule, so I thought I'd drive around the small town I had read so much about.

Today, Marshall has about twelve thousand residents. Farming is still a strong economic factor; corn, soybeans, and wheat are the chief crops, but the biggest single employer in town is ConAgra, the frozen-food giant. Its authoritative building (located on Banquet Drive, no less) and corrugated silos rise up to dominate the skyline of this historic town. When the residential neighborhoods come into view, one can travel in time from early 1970s ramblers and split-levels to the late nineteenth century. Passing by a Pizza Hut, the Wood and Huston Bank, and a video store, the drive gives way to more aesthetic older buildings, to the Marshall I'd seen in my mind when imagining its early years.

Coming into town via Arrow Street, the driver is led directly to the First Baptist Church, a commanding piece of architecture that draws the traffic to it, the Emerald City that is the exclamation point at the end of the yellow brick road. The road turns to the left, to continue in a rectangular route around the centrally placed historic Saline County courthouse; it is amazingly regal, its pressed red-brick face and limestone trim draw attention like a red dress at a quaint summer luncheon. A perimeter of shops surround it—Marshall Sport, Red Cross Pharmacy, their historic facades giving a vivid illustration of the place that the Jacksons would have visited on those special days when they ventured into town.

The library was easy enough to find, its large waving flag peeking over the trees in the square, a beacon drawing bibliophiles to the unassuming building at its base. Marvin Whilhite welcomed me to Marshall with a hearty handshake and a slow, soft-spoken drawl. A stocky gentleman probably in his early sixties, his blue-plaid shirt was meticulously pressed and his slightly graying hair crisply parted to one side and slicked down neatly. I imagined that he approached every day with a work ethic that left little room for improvement.

"Well, I think you're going to be pleased with what I've found," he said, beaming at piles of folders and papers stacked on the table in a side room. We browsed through the plat maps, school enrollment forms, property deeds, and dozens of other Pennytown materials. I asked Marvin not just about the tiny hamlet east of his town, but about his work as Marshall historian. I thought that, at this point in my journey, no one could be more enthusiastic about local Missouri history than I was. Not so. As he talked about his hobby, Marvin's eyes sparkled at his obvious pride in his work and the local recognition his interest brought him.

"I've been doing this kind of thing for thirty-four years," he told me. "I started by researching family, then branched out to local history."

A lifelong resident of Marshall, Marvin retired from the ConAgra plant a few years earlier, then let his interest in the region fill up more and more of his free time. His hobby soon turned into a passion and before long, he was a member of the Marshall Historical Society's board, a fact about which he absolutely beams. And so when I had given him the assignment to gather as much material on Pennytown as he could, he did so with childlike enthusiasm, gathering everything he could find on the subject. Together we combed through the handwritten notes, photos, and recorded personal memories in the collection with a near euphoria of fascination.

"Black people were turned out into the world after the Civil War and told 'fend for yourself,'" he said at one point. "They had a really hard life." He explained the special nature of the small community of Pennytown, not just its communal culture and self-sufficiency but the unique perspective Pennytowners had of themselves. "They were 'better' than others because the *owned* their land," he said, almost in a whisper. This gave the village a sense of being its own island, an oasis of confident living that stood apart from the rest of post–Civil War Southern black culture.

I gave Marvin a letter from the Clayton Jackson McGhie Memorial Committee to be placed on file for Jackson descendants and a compact disk of images from the memorial unveiling. I thanked him for his generosity, said goodbye and, armed with a rough copy of a recent plat map, I turned back onto the highway in search of the only structure remaining in Pennytown, the Freewill Baptist Church.

The ochre fields seemed to roll in every direction and as I wound up the dirt road, I traced the line on the map, trying to keep my car in synch with my finger. The bold intersection marked on the paper was much more prominent than the actual crossing and I absent-mindedly drove through it, continuing past the old farms and fields of what had been Blackwater Township a century ago. My frustration at missing the turn was calmed by the realization that even though I hadn't found the church yet, I was surrounded by a history worthy of contemplation. Though the trails and paths had long since grown over, I found that if I allowed myself, I could almost hear the singing of men on their way home from the fields and see thin streams of wood smoke rising in distance.

I turned around and made a sharp left, and the tiny shoebox of a building popped into view. At the crest of a slight hill, positioned near the gravel drive like it had been placed there for show, sat the Pennytown Freewill Baptist Church, its masonry blocks radiating a warm red against the backdrop of the yellow grassy fields. I pulled off the road, climbed out of the car, and wandered around the hallowed church grounds. The cows roaming the property were curious and very interested in this human standing near their fence; they sauntered over to me and I pulled a clump of grass from the ground, offering it to them. I don't really know much about cows, but the horses I've encountered always seem to appreciate an offer of grass. These cows couldn't have cared less.

Beyond the church, at the base of a gentle sloping hill, lay the former baptismal pond. I'd always imagined it tucked away more privately, surrounded by trees, cattails, and tall grasses. This pond almost looked to be man-made, a simple oval in the middle of a large clearing, no vegetation other than cropped field grass at its banks. I leaned against a tree, trying to imagine the day that Elmer would have fallen back into the dark water, the preacher's hand gently supporting the small of his back, Elmer's parents proudly giving thanks for their son's salvation.

The bark of the tree rubbed rough against my back; I reached up and felt its craggy branches, these ancient arms outstretched in a proud testament as the sole witness remaining to the wonderful existence that once surrounded it.

I'd seen the trees almost everywhere I'd driven, singular entities rising up from the plain like solitary sentries watching over the vast grasslands that surround them. Their thorny crowns spread outward wildly, occasional clumps appearing like spots in and among the branches. Nests, I'd assumed, hidden in the thickets of spring foliage, helplessly exposed in the late winter chill. I'd also assumed that they were oaks, only because their trunks and branches had struck me as oaklike. Besides, my lack of expertise in the area of botany had given me just a half dozen possibilities from which to choose. I discovered later that this tree overlooking the church was not an oak at all but what locals call the hedge-apple. And it has quite an interesting story.

Also called an Osage orange, the hedge-apple is apparently an incredibly resilient and sturdy tree. It began its native life in western Arkansas, southern Oklahoma, and eastern Texas; early explorers described the plant growing near the Osage native villages (hence the name) and it was reported that the wood of the tree was so valued that tribes would go to war over lands that were heavily planted with them. It's one of the heaviest woods on the continent; it's no wonder that bows made from the branch wood are legend.

So in demand were the Osage orangewood bows that an example of a bartered trade might be a horse and blanket or, by one report, "a comely young squaw." Osage bows have been found across the states, among the Shawnee and Wyandotte Indians in Ohio and the Blackfoot nations in Montana—nearly two thousand miles from their origins.

The early settlers found a more practical use for this handy tree. Besides utilizing the wood for tools, wagon parts, railroad ties, bridge pilings, and the like, farmers discovered a welcome benefit in the strange characteristics of the plant's growth. When planted one foot apart in a line, the trees will grow to yield a fence; limbs can be woven together to form an impenetrable force, the threatening thorny branches creating a barrier that is "horse-high, bull-strong, and hog-tight." For prairie wildlife accustomed to roaming freely, far out of reach of tree-perching predators, the hedge apple would prove all-too deadly.

Only when barbed wire was introduced in 1874 as a cheaper, more easily managed method did the tree's reputation as the darling of farm America fall off. By then, though, the tree had been planted in all 48 contiguous states—counties in northeast and northwest Missouri alone had over 2,000 miles of planted hedgerows. Even as it found its branches no longer in demand, the trunks were put to good use as fence posts for the very thing that had usurped the hedge. The wood from the tree is unique in that that it contains both antifungal and antioxidant compounds, protecting it from decay, so Osage orange posts that were set in the ground over fifty years ago still stand strong today—much like the tiny church over which the Pennytown trees stand. Sturdy and steadfast, in spite of the changing world around them. And this is what made me smile, that this odd, crusty tree with its thorny branches and its refusal to be forgotten should stand over the grounds where Elmer Jackson lived and played.

If ever there was an odd fruit to be borne, the hedge apple has it. Another common name for the tree is "mock orange" because of its very nature of deception. From a distance, once the fruit has changed in color from lime green to deep yellow, it does indeed look like a citrus fruit. Upon closer inspection, though, it reveals its true face. Taking a more cerebral form, its surface is a convoluted landscape of wrinkles and bumps that looks not unlike a tiny spherical brain.

What's even more intriguing is that this growth isn't so much a fruit in and of itself, but a collection of about 300 tiny fruits amassed into one round entity. Were it not for squirrels and the occasional deer, its seeds would remain untouched; unlike most fruits, which count on birds and animals to carry their seeds for propagation, the fruit of the Osage orange is bitter and uninviting to most.

Attempts to break apart the seed packs often end with great regret for the holder. An opened hedge apple releases an unpleasant milky white sap, creating a sticky adhesive to which dirt, debris and any other unwanted substance clings stubbornly. In some instances, the syrupy mess acts as an irritant, leaving a case of dermatitis in its wake. Months later, when I would attain one of these to eviscerate with my own hands, I came to understand all too well the nature of this mess. I thought I might remove the seeds from the pulp, dry them out and propagate them. I wondered whether or not I could grow Osage Orange seedlings, plant the trees on my own property. In doing this, I would then have a piece of Pennytown in my own backyard, a reminder of my undying connection to Elmer's roots.

At first cut, the center of the fruit oozed like a certain poison, gluey and thick over my gloved hands, changing rapidly to a sickly yellow coating that even a scrub of soapy water wouldn't cut. By the time I finished separating out what seemed like an endless number of tiny seeds, I had no choice but to simply discard the knife. And the small bit of fluid that had found its way onto my bare skin, while eventually scrubbed clean, left an oddly sweet odor like melon crossed with pumpkin that hung in the air for hours.

*   *   *

As I stood at the crest of the hill behind the Pennytown Freewill Baptist Church, I felt overwhelmed with emotion. What was I doing here, thousands of miles from home, in the coldness of February in the middle of a cow pasture? What had I hoped to achieve by visiting the hometown of the man whom my great-grandfather helped kill?

I'd wanted to find answers, even if I wasn't quite sure what the questions were. The truth was, my entire journey up to this point—from the initial discovery of the lynchings to this moment under the hedge-apple tree—had been one of contrasts. Facing the differences between what had been my family's perception of our past and Duluth's vision of my family, I had been desperately seeking to find the reality that lay between. Here in the space that once had been Pennytown, Elmer's childhood haven, I struggled to hold the silence and serenity up against the screams of thousands and the blood of three. And the irony that was my very presence here shook me to the core. We were linked in spirit, my great-grandfather and I, as I reached down to feel the dirt that lay beneath the tree, near the spot where a beautiful child had been born. That child entered the world where I now stood apologetic and atoning; the man he would become would leave the world where my great-grandfather stood complicit and heartless. Blood spilled, blood connected, and the stain of strange fruit that might never come clean.

CHAPTER 32

T HE STRANGE THING ABOUT combing through history is that you can only find what the teeth manage to catch. As long as something is there, provided someone has taken the time to record the details for someone, someday to unearth, it will happen. But if your steps are weightless or your footprints covered too well there may be no indication that you ever walked this planet. It's a great frustration that lingers, even after this long journey, that the lives and histories of Isaac McGhie and Elias Clayton remain a mystery to me. And I fear that by sharing Elmer Jackson's story, I have eclipsed their faces even more, pushing them further into obscurity. Perhaps one day, I will find that one clue that will open up their lives to me. Until then, I know I may celebrate what I have achieved.

Enough tracks were made for me to have pieced together a reasonable picture of one family in this epic saga. Census data, recorded histories, directories, and newspaper articles showed that the Jacksons did, in fact, exist. More than that, they led fascinating, meaningful lives while they were here.

* * *

Virginia Huston was the last person born in Pennytown, on December 8, 1944. The current caretaker and fund-raiser for the Freewill Baptist Church, she is one of the key coordinators of the annual gathering of descendants that takes place there each August. Unfortunately, I wouldn't come in contact with Virginia until after my initial visit to Missouri. I found her name in the midst of my continued research on the small church and we'd communicated via e-mail for a few weeks before I was able to phone her to talk more about the Duluth-Pennytown connection.

It was late, well after ten in the evening, when we finally spoke. Besides working two jobs, she explained, she did a lot of volunteering, so a late call was not only acceptable, it was necessary. Her voice radiated a warmth and interest that I could feel instantly. "This is important," she said. We talked for some time about my journey to that point, of the challenges I'd had trying to connect with Elmer's family. She understood the difficulties I'd had and would likely continue to experience. "Some people might not want to hear bad news," she said, but she quickly agreed that history had to be put out there, accessible, so that others might learn from the events of the past.

Virginia explained her relationship to Pennytown. Her mother, Josephine Lawrence, had been instrumental in getting the church restored before her death. While the land was currently owned by a huge research farm, the church itself had been placed on the National Register of Historic Places in 1988 and rebuilt and restored in 1996. There were many Pennytowners still in the area, she said, including the oldest living descendant, Ella Wright-Lewis.

"My mother had a lot of fond memories of Pennytown," says Virginia. "When she was in attendance at Thornlea School, she got into trouble and her teacher, he had her stand on one leg and (later) write a report on Pennytown." Josephine interviewed former residents, and the project took on a life of its own. She became intent on preserving both the memory and physical structure of the church, eventually becoming a respected authority on the historical town.

Virginia joyfully told me stories that her mother had shared with her, tales that were familiar to me from my previous readings. She recalled her great-great-grandfather Blackwater Jim Jackson, who was a wizard with the fishing rod and shared his bounty generously with other townspeople. She told me of the neighboring Finnis Creek Cemetery and the funeral customs that were typical of the "old Baptist ways." The deceased would lie in state for a week, for honoring, visitation, and revelry before taking his final ride in the horse and buggy to his eternal resting place.

Virginia is a very distant relative of Elmer (her aunt had married Elmer's cousin). She confirmed many of the assumptions I'd made about the Jackson men—James, Aaron, and Thomas—who shared the small plot of land with Clifton and Rachel. "Oh, they were brothers," she said. "If their ages were close and they lived next door to one another, I'm sure of it." This meant that the Jackson children who showed up on the school rolls well into the 1920s were Elmer's cousins and their children. This also meant that there were indeed Jackson descendants still living in and around Marshall. Before we hung up, I asked her if she had told anyone else about what I was doing, what I had discovered about one of the Pennytown children. "I tell people every day," she said without hesitation. Her voice was authoritative and resolute. "I know sometimes people don't like to be reminded of the bad things that happen, but this is part of history. We have to tell it like is and maybe it can be a healing process for everyone."

CHAPTER 33

I NEVER SAW MY GRANDFATHER READ. I saw him write only once—he'd signed his name with an X on a delivery clipboard and I'd been impressed. Only in the movies had I ever seen that audacious act. My mother can recall watching her daddy fish through the daily newspaper, scanning the obituary section for the names of the funeral homes handling that week's services. If he saw Swedberg's, he knew he'd have work that day.

For several years, my grandfather worked as a gravedigger. He dug graves to bury people he'd known, men he'd worked with and for, men he drank with. The weedy, unkempt grounds of the Edmonds Cemetery was the final resting place of Edmonds's working class, and my grandfather knew that one day he and his family would lie under the grasses on which he walked. He'd planned for this, securing a half-dozen plots in the middle of the park, ensuring that even if his family couldn't have a permanent home in life, they would in death.

Every now and then, my grandfather would get a call for a burial that might not have been listed in the obituaries. He'd drive his truck to the cemetery, parking near the back of the office away from the main drive, unload his pick and shovel, and amble to the small lawn behind the picket fencing. In a few hours, a single box would arrive. Sometimes there would be a name attached, too often the last name would simply read "Doe." This was the potter's field, where the anonymous were laid to rest, the men and women whose departures from the earth would be noticed by nobody.

It was with a sad irony, then, that it would take my mother and me over twenty years to finally put money aside to mark her parents' and grandfather's graves. It just hadn't been a priority for us, really. We'd had car payments to make, tuition to pay, and the idea of spending our hard-earned money to put a piece of marble in the ground seemed superfluous. During this period of rediscovery of our family we awoke to the sudden acute need to give our family the acknowledgement they deserved. "We were here, here we lie," is all that any of us wants, after all. And I knew then that it couldn't end there. I'd have to go back, return to Pennytown and speak with the Jacksons. It was time to complete the circle, to stand face to face with them and let them know that Elmer's departure did matter, it had been felt and acknowledged by more people than they could ever imagine.

*   *   *

The colors along the road to Pennytown were more brilliant than when I'd come the first time. What had been stalks of smoky grays and browns was now a vibrant landscape of life; the tans and greens of the lush cornfields were muted only by the thin layer of road dust covering my windshield. Waves of heat danced off the hood of the rental car and I checked the dashboard to see what the outside temperature had reached: 105 degrees. I'd watched the weather reports for Missouri before coming, although I'd known that August in the Midwest would likely be hot. It was the summer of 2006, and the whole country had been in the midst of a heat wave, so I hadn't held up my hopes for a reprieve when it came time for me to go. I turned at the first intersection I came to and climbed the familiar hill to the Pennytown Freewill Baptist Church. Coming up over the crest, a collection of cars came into view, as did a small group of about twenty people gathered in the shade of the canopy of the Osage orange.

The previous year, Virginia Huston had invited me to the annual gathering at Pennytown. On the first Sunday of August, she'd explained, descendants of Pennytown residents came together to reminisce, worship, and celebrate the memory of Pennytown. It was her feeling that there would be a place for me there. I'd not been ready at the time of the first invitation. There was too much for me to sort out and when the reality of meeting kin of the Jackson families faced me, I stepped back. For all the time I'd spent looking for a connection, I had no idea what I could or should do.

As I pulled the car up onto the grass next to the others, I gathered my materials from the passenger seat: photos, my camera, a sticky blackberry cobbler I'd picked up from a Cracker Barrel restaurant just off the highway on the way from Kansas City. A screened tent stood near the gathering and a couple of figures moved in and around the tables that had been set up inside. The heat smacked me in the face when I got out of the car; I remembered to slow my movements to half speed as I wandered to the tent with my dessert. Several folks looked up from their conversations, taking notice of the first white face to arrive. A middle-aged man broke from the small group with whom he'd been standing and bounded over to me, hand outstretched. A few others waved hellos and I motioned back as I fumbled with the zipper on the tent.

"Are you Warren?" a voice behind me asked. I turned around to see a woman somewhat shorter than I, whose hair was cropped even more closely than mine. Her round face beamed a broad smile that radiated expectant warmth. "I'm Virginia." We exchanged hearty "hellos" and an eager handshake, the kind of greeting that comes from months of anticipation. "I recognized your voice," she said. I fumbled a comment about standing out from the crowd, which Virginia returned with gentle assurances that the crowd would be getting much bigger. As we made our way back to the group, she pointed to a table at the far end of the gathering. "Those are some Jacksons over there." I stood where I was, staring nervously at the half dozen or so people seated at a collection of picnic tables just down the hill from me, not sure what might need to happen next. The introductions had to come from me, I knew, but I really had no idea what I should do. After all this time—two years of contemplation—I was no closer to a plan than I had been at the beginning. I took a deep breath and moved down the hill toward the group.

I had my notebook in hand, ready to scratch notes. I'd decided that I would explain my reasons for being there later and just be vague about my interest in Pennytown. A buzz had started earlier that I had come to write an article and unless I was asked specifically, I let it go. Those who wanted more information were assured that I'd be sharing later. As I reached the Jackson table, I simply sat down and began asking questions, nodding knowledgeably when a familiar surname came out.

"Have you been coming to these for awhile?" I asked one woman. She told me yes, that she had been several times. "May I ask you your surname?"

"Williams," she said. "My name is Remi Williams."

My stomach began to tingle as I remembered that Elmer's grandmother's maiden name was Williams. "Ah yes," I said, looking through my stack of papers. "I know the Williams name. Christine Williams was married to Mack Jackson."

"My grandmother is a Jackson," she said, pointing to an elderly woman seated next to her. "Her name is Mary Clariette Jackson."

This whole time, Mary had sat quietly as I'd asked questions around her. I'd been surprised to hear she was the woman's grandmother—her smooth skin belied her years and even when she told me she was eighty-five years old, her family members guffawed and began flashing hands at me to indicate that she was well over. Mary told me that her grandparents were Richard Green and his wife Elizabeth, but that her "natural" grandfather had been Tom Jackson. I felt a sudden wave of emotion wash over me and I struggled to maintain a semblance of calm. I took in a sharp breath. From what I had pieced together, it would appear that Mary's father had been Elmer's cousin.

I kept talking with her, continuing the conversation and trying to keep control of the conflicting feelings that were welling up inside of me. I knew that I was deceiving her (and the others), playing the nonchalant interviewer, yet I also knew that the most inappropriate thing I could do at that moment was to reveal the real reason I was there. *I'm not a legacy of life in Pennytown, I'm a legacy of death.* I'd been moving comfortably

189

in a groove and suddenly, I had no idea why I had come at all. It hit me at last that in my efforts to shake my own family tree, I was about to shake theirs as well. And they hadn't asked for it.

"Can you please tell me, Mrs. Jackson, one of your fondest memories about Pennytown?" I asked Mary.

Sitting up straight in her seat, she announced proudly, "I used to sing solos here in the church." She smiled broadly and planted her cane firmly in the dirt. "This is my home church," she said, nodding toward the tiny chapel.

"You went to church here?" a voice called out behind her. Mary nodded intently.

"Is that the old baptismal pond?" I turned and pointed to the circle of water behind the gathering, just down the slight hill from the church. A four-foot extension of drainage pipe jutted out from the bank of the pond. The thick layer of algae bloom was, like the rest of us, a colorful summer visitor. Mary nodded and told me that she had indeed been baptized in the pond as a child.

"Oh yeah." All around her, family and friends nodded, laughing. "Even the cows won't go in there, now."

I smiled and brought the conversation back to a name she'd mentioned. "You said your grandfather was Dick Green." Some months earlier, I'd received materials from the Josephine Lawrence (Virginia's mother) Collection held at the University of Missouri. I remembered a picture from the collection, a photo of a young boy sitting on the porch of a shack that had been identified as Dick Green's home. I reached under my seat for the envelope, bringing it to my lap and fishing out the image. "Have you seen this?" I asked Mary, handing it to her.

"No, I haven't," she said, leaning forward. She took it from me gingerly, hands trembling just slightly as she drew it close to her face. Her eyes squinted, her brow tightening as she studied the rough picture. Suddenly her hand dropped to her chest and she gasped. "It's my granddad's house!"

A woman behind her lunged forward, peering over her shoulder. "Mama," the woman exclaimed, "that's your daddy settin' there on the porch!"

Mary pulled the photo even closer, so close that her nose nearly touched the paper, and gazed at it a few more seconds. "Oh, yes," she said matter-of-factly, her finger tracing the image of the small boy. "It is."

For a brief moment, we sat in silence, each taking in the power of the moment. Mary, I imagined, was touching a part of her past that she'd long forgotten, soaking in the beauty of an unexpected treat. I was basking in a moment of small redemption, of realizing a tiny gift that I'd been able to give to an old woman who likely hadn't planned to find anything more on this day than old friends, good food, and lively prayer. I told her she could keep the photo, and that I'd send copies to her family. "Oh, what a treasure," she sang quietly, holding it close to her chest. "What a treasure."

I decided it was time to leave the Jacksons alone and did so, hoping that I would be able to talk more with them later, after I shared my Duluth connection with everyone. A plate of fried chicken, Cajun potato salad, and a tempting slice of brown-sugar pie awaited me as I planted myself at the picnic table. Across from me a woman ate quietly, stealing looks at me as I ate with one hand and scribbled in my notebook with the other. When our eyes met, she smiled shyly and said hello. I asked her if she'd been to the homecoming before.

"No," she said. "My dad always gets invitations for this and I decided to come this time." She introduced herself as Donna and told me that she lived nearby and had been to see the church, but had never come to the reunion. When I asked about her surname, she smiled and tilted her head down.

"It's listed in the records as Madison, but that's just what my great-grandfather said," she explained. Looking around, she lowered her voice just a bit. "He was a full-blooded Indian, but we don't know what tribe. We're not even sure where he got the name from." She went on to explain that her great-grandfather would never tell his true lineage, much to his offspring's disappointment. When he had been asked about it, he'd grown uncomfortable and would change the subject. "I have my suspicions about why he would never tell," she said, leaning in closer to me. "I think he ran away from his reservation and came to Pennytown. And he knew that if anyone found out where he was from, they'd take him back."

I was struck by the parallel that had suddenly formed between us, both of us seeking to find truth in our own ancestry, both struggling with the frustration of shameful silence. "How does this make you feel, to have this secret for all these years?" I asked.

"It's disappointing," she said, shaking her head. "I'm not angry, but I feel sometimes like I've been cheated." Still, she explained, she tries to keep things in perspective. "We don't understand it, but then we didn't live in their times. We're trying to make sense out of it through today's eyes."

*   *   *

We sat, dozens of us, in the pews of the Freewill Baptist Church as music thundered around us. In front of the congregation, a slender man stamped his foot and clapped, leading the group in a rousing chorus.

I feel better, hallelujah!
So much, better, hallelujah!
So much, better, hallelujah!
Since I laid my burdens down.

The heat intensified with the compact bodies and the confines of four walls. The single fan fronting the pulpit swirled the thick, damp air and I began to wonder if the paddle fans working back and forth in front of the faces, mine included, served more to generate body heat by exertion than to create any real relief. For a quick moment I thought of Elmer, and the last night of his life; the stifling heat, the claustrophobia, no relief in sight. I looked around the room at the joy and love and imagined it replaced with terror and hatred, the celebration of life replaced by a call for death. I listened to the gospel singing, the peaceful songs, and wondered if Elmer heard these in his final moments, even hummed them to himself as he sat amid the sounds of the cell walls breaking in around him.

"Warren Read?"

I snapped back to the present; I was being invited up by the preacher to share my story, my purpose for being there. I hadn't prepared a speech this time. I figured I'd told the tale enough times I could recite it in my sleep. As I began to talk, to explain my journey, the lynchings, the connection between Elmer and Pennytown, I felt the flood of the experience wash over me and my throat clamped shut. I paused, took a breath, and looked into the eyes of those facing me. Dozens of deep brown eyes bored into me and I remembered the faces of the mob, the myriad expressions staring back from the postcard as I searched for my great-grandfather and for an instant I imagined that they hated me, that more than anything they wanted my tainted soul off the premises. And then, a connection.

A woman, a beautiful, black woman under the graceful shade of a lacey wide-brimmed hat, smiled at me, a knowing smile of deep, shared pain. She nodded slowly as I struggled to find my words and her eyes spoke a freeing empathy that drew me out of my fear. I spoke to her and she accepted my testimony without question.

I explained how I'd propagated trees from a collection of acorns and hedge-apples that Virginia had sent me. I had shared the story with my own church congregation and we sold the tiny Pennytown trees to raise funds to help maintain the Pennytown church, the proceeds of which I presented to Virginia.

"If there is an element of my being that was instrumental in bringing death," I explained, "then I believe I have a responsibility to help make a wrong act right." I told them I hoped that by cultivating the trees, by bringing Elmer's story beyond the postcard, I would encourage life where there had been only death. In addition, I hoped to bring the last of the oak saplings to Duluth, where a Pennytown tree would at last be planted at Elmer's grave.

There were heartfelt amens and hallelujahs and when I returned to my seat, the preacher, a powerful man who described himself as "from the old school" (he was wearing a suit in a room filled with shirtsleeves and shorts) took the pulpit.

"I want to thank you, Brother Read," he began. "There are a lot of young folks today who don't appreciate what went on in our history. I grew up in Mississippi," he continued, his face growing ever more serious and somber, "and I remember when those things happened. It's important to never forget."

After the benediction, the crowd made its way out the door, into the coolness of the hundred-degree air. Some people moved to their vehicles to make their way home. A few people came to talk with me and right away I was struck by the peculiar notion that they were intent on assuaging the guilt that they imagined was weighing down my soul. "These things happened," they said. "It was a different time." "It's important to remember that even today people get caught up in the moment," one woman told me. "It's an easy thing to have happen." I thanked her, gently refusing to allow her to let me off the hook.

"Thankfully, we don't often see lynchings like this anymore," I told the woman. "But just because we don't see physical lynchings doesn't mean it's not happening in other ways." She looked at me knowingly. "The roots of hatred, anger, and violence are all still there," I said. "It's important to own it and part of owning it is embracing its history."

Before long, the lawn sat emptied of people, the dozens of cars vanished from the grounds. Platters were put away, litter had been stuffed into overflowing bags, and I looked around, lamenting the fact that the Jacksons had left before I could talk with them further. In spite of all that had taken place, I still had a feeling of incompleteness. I neurotically imagined that they'd had no desire to talk with me whatsoever, that I'd been an embarrassment, a presumptuous buffoon who'd hit them with the unthinkable and expected them to run to me with outstretched, forgiving arms. It was more likely that these people simply had no idea what they could possibly say. Could I blame them? After all, I'd had three years to think it over and I still hadn't figured out the right words.

Within a week of this initial meeting, though, I would at last make contact with Don Claret, Mary Clariette Jackson's son. As promised, I'd sent him the photo of Dick Green's house, with my apologies for not being honest with them at our meeting, sharing my understanding of the awkwardness they must have felt toward me that day. The next morning, I received an e-mail reply from Don:

Hello Warren,

It was a pleasure to meet you in Pennytown. This was my first trip there with my mother (Mary Clariette Jackson). I found the research that you are conducting and the story told at the church to be

incredible. I do hope to visit Duluth now and to look for the
memorial site there. If you are ever in Minneapolis or passing
through on your way up to Duluth please give me a ring. A dinner,
chat, and progress report might be in order. Thanks for sharing.
My mother was VERY SURPRISED as well as myself.

On the way to my car, I stopped to say goodbye to Virginia as she was bidding farewell to a friend. "I'll see you soon, now," she'd told her. She turned to me and threw out her arms to embrace me. "Thank you so much for coming," she said into my ear. "I know it was emotional for you to talk about it."

"That happens sometimes," I said. "I'm fine until I'm in the moment." I looked around at the grounds once more, at the church, the pond, the craggy old trees of Pennytown. "I guess it was just being on this site, sur- rounded by all these people. I can't help but picture folks in that church a hundred years ago, before all that happened." My mind clouded and I struggled to put into words what I was feeling—that the mood today had mirrored what I imagined was Elmer's world once upon a time, and how no one ever could have imagined the cruel violence that would one day visit itself upon someone from a place so safe and secure.

Virginia smiled again and nodded. "I know it's not easy for people to hear this. They like to sweep things under the bed and forget about them, but you can't do that."

"It's about responsibility," I told her. "For me, anyway. I grew up with people in my life who refused take responsibility for anything. Like you said, they wanted to keep things hidden away, under the bed."

"Yeah, yeah," she nodded.

"I just think we all have a responsibility to take the good and bad things that have been laid before us," I continued, "and make them work for today."

"Amen," she said, reaching out and hugging me again. "Amen. I hope you'll come back to see us again."

As I drove away from the church, a cloud of dust filling the rectangle of my rearview mirror, I wondered if I ever would return to Pennytown. I suspect that I won't, though in some way I feel that I must—if not in person, then in spirit. From Duluth to Topeka to Pennytown, my roots have spread. I'm connected to these places, if not by blood then by an unexpected destiny, and those places, like the ground beneath a wide-reaching oak, feed my limbs by the mere circumstance of my having planted myself there.

*   *   *

When I arrived home the next day, Shayne was eager to hear about my trip. He listened intently, but at the first break in the story, he interrupted. "By the way, the morning glory is coming up in your garden again," he warned. "You need to get it before it goes to seed." During the garden rehab, we'd brought in a truckload of dirt from one of Shayne's clients, another garden that was receiving a makeover. Most of the dirt would go into the borders of my garden; the rest was used as fill for a new bed he was installing off of our front porch. "Something happened with the dirt," he'd said. We discovered too late that along with the soil came seeds of morning glory, a viciously invasive vine just waiting for the optimum conditions to sprout and take over.

I put away my luggage, rifled through the mail, and made my way to the garden. Kneeling down next to the roses, I carefully snapped the vines that had entwined themselves around the thorny stems, loosening the chokehold they had on the bush. Scraping deep down into the soil, I gripped the weeds at the roots and yanked them out. Something did happen. Like it or not, just like the morning glory in my garden, the lyncher in me exists, no longer buried, no longer entwining itself around things of beauty reaching for sunlight, but always trying. I can seek to control it; I can work to keep it from spreading, but it will likely be there forever. Because in my garden, as in my life, something always happens. That, I cannot deny.

ACKNOWLEDGMENTS

There are so many people without whose support this book would never have reached completion. First and foremost, my sincere thanks to my partner Shayne, whose willingness to take on my share of parenting responsibilities, be my worst critic and best supporter kept me going at moments when I was ready to settle for less than my best. Also, much gratitude to my mother-in-law Barb, for being a willing reader and ardent cheerleader. To my editor at Borealis Books, Pam McClanahan, who believed in this project before it was even close to its present incarnation—I give my utmost gratitude. Her critical eye and effusive praise managed to keep me in love with the book, even on those days when I was ready to throw it in the bin. Thank you to Michael Fedo and Heidi Bakk-Hansen, whose generosity helped clear much of the undergrowth in order that I might make my own path. To Rebecca Walker, whose guidance and faith in this project and my abilities helped bring me to a product of which I could be proud. To Virginia Huston, whose unconditional support and understanding allowed me to believe that what I was doing was right. To the many researchers and resources on the periphery: Marvin Wilhite, Sonny Scroggins, Craig Grau, Ken Olsen, Grace Linden of the Sioux City Public Museum, Larry Obermeyer of the Siouxland Historical Railroad Association, and Jack R. Cox, who generously provided me a copy of the hard-to-find 97th tour of the Robinson Show route list. To the University of Missouri-Columbia, the Kansas State Historical Society, the Topeka Public Library, and the Minnesota Historical Society whose invaluable holdings allowed me to dig more deeply into the unknown. To my sister, Karen, and, most importantly, to my mother Nellie, whose unselfish honesty and openness allowed this to be not only a moving story, but a journey of healing.

REFERENCES

I would like to acknowledge the following sources for the research portions of this book:

The *New York Times* archives, the archives of the *Duluth News Tribune, The Plaindealer* and the *Topeka Daily Capitol,* among other newspapers. The books *The Lynchings in Duluth,* by Michael Fedo; *The Circus Age: Culture and Society Under the Big Top,* by Janet M. Davis; *Wagon Show Days,* by Gil Robinson; *Give 'em a John Robinson,* by Richard E. Conover, and *A History of the Hemp Industry in Kentucky,* by James F. Hopkins. "Missouri Slave Data," http://www.missouri-slave-data.org/ and "African Missouri," a collection of articles and holdings from the University of Missouri–St. Louis were very informative in helping me understand the unique nature and identities of upland slavery; "The Josephine Lawrence Collection," University of Missouri–Columbia, provided a wealth of precious information about Pennytown and its inhabitants. In addition to each of these resources, I utilized countless documents, articles, and letters from the holdings of the Minnesota Historical Society, the Kansas State Historical Society, and the Duluth and Topeka Public Libraries.

The Lyncher in Me was designed and set in Minion type
by Christopher Kuntze, Whitefield, New Hampshire.
Printed by Friesens, Altona, Manitoba.